NAVIGATING LEADERSHIP FRAMEWORKS

PRACTICAL APPLICATIONS FOR LEADERS

MANDEEP SINGH

Copyright © Mandeep Singh 2024
All Rights Reserved.

ISBN 979-8-89363-927-8

Contents

Acknowledgement

Writing this book has been a deeply enriching journey, and I am grateful for the support and inspiration I have received from many individuals and sources.

First and foremost, I would like to express my heartfelt gratitude to my family. My wife, Jaspreet, and my children, Samar and Gunisha, have been my pillars of strength throughout this process. Thank you for your unwavering support and understanding during the countless nights and weekends that went into writing this book.

I am also deeply appreciative of the guidance and mentorship from my seniors and bosses at the various organizations where I have had the privilege to work: BBC, Sterling Holidays, Rentokil India, Tattva Home Healthcare, and my current organization, Casagrand Premier Builders Ltd. Each of you has contributed to my growth and understanding of leadership in unique and invaluable ways. A special thanks to all my colleagues who have shared their insights and experiences, helping me to become a better leader.

This book would not have been possible without the foundational work of numerous authors and researchers who have developed and refined the leadership frameworks discussed within these pages. Your contributions have been instrumental in shaping my understanding and have provided the building blocks for this book. Thank you for your dedication to advancing the field of leadership.

I would also like to acknowledge the incredible support of ChatGPT, developed by OpenAI, which played a significant role in helping me articulate my thoughts and compile this book. The advanced capabilities of ChatGPT made the writing process more efficient and effective, allowing me to focus on the content and insights I wanted to share.

Finally, I am grateful to you, the reader, for embarking on this journey with me. It is my hope that this book serves as a valuable resource in your own leadership journey, helping you to navigate the complexities of leadership with confidence and insight.

Content Summary

Welcome to "Navigating Leadership Frameworks – Practical Applications for Leaders." In this book, we embark on a journey to explore a diverse array of leadership frameworks, each offering valuable insights and perspectives to empower individuals on their leadership journey.

Beginning with classic theories such as the Great Man Theory and Trait Theory, we delve into the foundational principles that have shaped our understanding of leadership over the years. From there, we move on to explore contemporary approaches including Behavioral Theories, Transformational Leadership, and Servant Leadership, each offering unique perspectives on effective leadership in today's dynamic world.

Throughout the book, we provide practical insights, real-world examples, and actionable strategies to help readers apply these frameworks in their own leadership roles. Whether you're a seasoned executive, an aspiring leader, or a student of leadership theory, this book offers something valuable for everyone.

Our underlying message is clear: effective leadership is not a one-size-fits-all endeavor. By understanding and leveraging the various frameworks presented in this book, individuals can develop their own unique leadership style and approach, tailored to their strengths, values, and the needs of their organization.

Join us as we explore the rich tapestry of leadership frameworks and discover how they can guide us on the path to becoming more effective and impactful leaders.

Introduction

Leadership is more than a role; it's a journey that intertwines with the fabric of our professional and personal lives. As a seasoned finance professional with over 20 years of experience, a Chartered Accountant, and an alumnus of the esteemed ISB, my own journey has been a testament to the transformative power of effective leadership.

Over the course of more than two decades in the finance arena, I've come to realize that leadership is not just a professional role; it's an ongoing odyssey of growth and adaptation. As a Chartered Accountant, I've delved into the intricacies of financial landscapes, deciphering the language of numbers, and steering organizations through fiscal challenges. My journey at the ISB added a strategic layer, providing insights into the broader dynamics that shape businesses.

In the dynamic and fast-paced world of finance, decisions are not mere choices; they are pivotal moments that reverberate throughout an entire organization. Leadership is not a luxury; it's an absolute necessity. The responsibility of navigating complexities, making impactful decisions, and inspiring teams falls squarely on the shoulders of those in leadership roles.

Leadership, in the financial realm, is an art—a delicate dance that requires finesse in navigating the intricate complexities of markets, regulations, and organizational dynamics. It's about steering through uncertainties, strategically positioning for success, and understanding that each decision holds the potential to shape the financial destiny of an organization.

In this intricate dance of leadership, frameworks emerge as guiding constellations, offering direction and structure amid the vast expanse of decision-making. They are the navigational tools that leaders use to chart their course, aligning their actions with a broader vision. For me, these frameworks have been like a compass, aiding me in making decisions that have lasting impacts on financial strategies and organizational outcomes.

As I take a thoughtful retrospective look at the trajectory of my professional journey, the profound influence of effective leadership becomes increasingly apparent. It transcends the conventional metrics of success and delves into the very heart of organizational culture, leaving an indelible mark on the dynamics that shape teams and outcomes.

Effective leadership, in its true essence, is not confined to the narrow pursuit of financial goals. While achieving fiscal objectives is undoubtedly crucial, the impact of leadership resonates far beyond the balance sheets. It extends into the intangible realms of organizational culture, manifesting in the creation of a vibrant and collaborative environment.

The transformative power of leadership lies in its ability to instill a culture characterized by collaboration, resilience, and innovation. It goes beyond the day-to-day operations and financial achievements, permeating the very ethos of the workplace. A leader, in this sense, becomes a catalyst for a collaborative spirit, fostering a collective resilience that propels the team forward in the face of challenges.

Innovation, a hallmark of effective leadership, flourishes in an environment where individuals feel empowered and encouraged to think creatively. Leaders who understand the significance of innovation not only drive organizational progress but also nurture a sense of fulfillment and purpose among team members.

Moreover, leadership's impact isn't limited to the organizational level; it intricately weaves into the professional growth and well-being of every member within the team. A leader's guidance and support contribute to the development of individuals, enabling them to reach their full potential. The cultivation of a positive work culture directly influences the overall well-being of team members, creating an environment where individuals feel valued, supported, and motivated.

In essence, effective leadership is a holistic force that shapes the very fabric of an organization. It's a force that extends its influence into the intangible aspects of culture, collaboration, and innovation, while simultaneously nurturing the growth and well-being of every individual within the team. As we explore various leadership frameworks in this journey, it is with the understanding that leadership is not merely a role; it is a profound and transformative influence that permeates every corner of the professional landscape.

In the chapters that follow, we will explore various leadership frameworks, unraveling their nuances, and delving into their practical applications. Through these frameworks, I aim to share insights, providing aspiring leaders with a toolkit that goes beyond theory—a toolkit forged in the crucible of real-world leadership.

Welcome to "Navigating Leadership Frameworks: Practical Applications for Leaders." Together, let's embark on a journey that transcends theory, embracing the practical artistry of leadership.

Chapter 1

Overview of Leadership Frameworks

Defining Leadership Frameworks

Leadership frameworks serve as invaluable tools in navigating the complexities of leadership. They are structured models that distill the multifaceted nature of effective leadership into key components. These components may include traits, behaviors, and situational factors, providing leaders with a systematic approach to understanding, analyzing, and improving their leadership practices.

Leadership frameworks are like maps for the complex terrain of leadership. Just as a map helps navigate through unfamiliar territory, leadership frameworks offer a structured approach to understanding the multifaceted nature of leadership. By breaking down leadership into manageable elements, frameworks provide leaders with a systematic way to analyze, evaluate, and enhance their leadership practices.

Consider a leader facing a challenge – without a framework, they might rely solely on intuition or past experiences. However, with a framework in hand, they gain a structured perspective. For example, trait-based frameworks might prompt them to reflect on their inherent strengths and weaknesses, while situational frameworks might guide them to consider the specific context in which they operate.

Components of Leadership Framework

1. **Trait based components:**

   - Some frameworks focus on inherent qualities that are believed to make individuals effective leaders. Traits such as integrity, decisiveness, and emotional intelligence are often highlighted.

   - Example: The "Great Man" theory from the 19th century suggests that leaders are born with innate qualities that set them apart. Individuals possessing these traits naturally rise to leadership positions.

2. **Behavioral components:**

   - Other frameworks emphasize observable behaviors exhibited by leaders. This can include communication styles, decision-making approaches, and how leaders interact with their teams.

   - Example: The Ohio State Studies in the 1940s identified two key leadership behaviors – consideration (relationship-oriented) and initiation of structure (task-oriented).

3. **Situational components:**

   - Recognizing the complexity of the change, the leader applies a situational leadership approach. They assess the readiness of team members to adapt to the change and adjust their leadership style accordingly – providing more guidance to those who need it and empowering those who are more capable.

By integrating these components, the leader creates a nuanced and adaptive leadership strategy tailored to the specific demands of the situation. This practical application showcases how leadership frameworks provide a structured and comprehensive approach for leaders to navigate the dynamic challenges they encounter in their roles.

Significance of Leadership Frameworks

Leadership frameworks play a pivotal role in shaping the way leaders think about, approach, and execute their roles. Their significance lies in providing a shared language and understanding that transcends individual experiences, fostering effective communication, collaboration, and overall organizational success.

Shared Understanding:

1. **Common Ground for Teams:**

   - Leadership frameworks act as a unifying force within teams. In a diverse workforce with individuals from various backgrounds and experiences, frameworks offer a common understanding of what constitutes effective leadership.
   - Example: Imagine a team with members from different cultural backgrounds. Leadership frameworks provide a shared set of principles, enabling team members to align their efforts and work towards common objectives, reducing misunderstandings and enhancing team cohesion.

2. **Consistent Organizational Culture:**

   - Frameworks contribute to the development of a consistent organizational culture. When leaders and team members share a common understanding of leadership principles, it promotes a cohesive culture that aligns with the organization's values and goals.

- Example: In an organization that values innovation, a leadership framework emphasizing transformational leadership may be adopted to encourage leaders to inspire creativity and adaptability among their teams.

Effective Decision-Making:

1. **Strategic Decision – Making:**

   - Leadership frameworks provide leaders with a strategic perspective, allowing them to make informed decisions aligned with organizational goals. By considering the principles embedded in these frameworks, leaders can navigate complex situations with clarity and purpose.
   - Example: A leader faced with a critical decision regarding a company restructuring may refer to leadership frameworks to assess the situation, considering both the traits required for effective leadership during change and the situational factors influencing the decision.

2. **Adaptability and Flexibility:**

   - In a rapidly changing world, adaptability is a key leadership trait. Frameworks encourage leaders to be flexible in their approaches, recognizing that what works in one situation may not be effective in another.
   - Example: A leader, well-versed in various leadership frameworks, can adapt their style to different contexts. For instance, during a period of crisis, they may shift towards a more directive approach (transactional leadership), whereas in times of stability, they may adopt a more empowering style (transformational leadership).

Enhanced Leadership Development:

1. **Structured Leadership Development:**

   - Leadership frameworks serve as a roadmap for leadership development programs. By understanding the components of effective leadership, organizations can design targeted development initiatives to cultivate the skills and behaviors essential for success.

   - Example: A leadership development program may incorporate modules on specific frameworks, allowing aspiring leaders to learn and practice the traits and behaviors associated with successful leadership.

2. **Continuous Improvement:**

   - The significance of leadership frameworks extends beyond initial training; they provide a basis for continuous improvement. Leaders can assess their strengths and weaknesses, identify areas for growth, and engage in ongoing development to enhance their leadership effectiveness.

   - Example: A leader, reflecting on feedback from their team and comparing it to leadership frameworks, may identify areas for improvement. This continuous feedback loop contributes to their ongoing growth and development as a leader.

In essence, the significance of leadership frameworks lies in their ability to create a common understanding, guide effective decision-making, foster adaptability, and serve as a foundation for leadership development. As leaders and organizations embrace these frameworks, they are better equipped to navigate the complexities of leadership and achieve sustainable success.

Evolution of Leadership Frameworks

The evolution of leadership frameworks reflects the dynamic nature of leadership theory and practice over time. From early attempts to identify inherent traits to contemporary models that emphasize situational and contextual factors, the journey of leadership frameworks has been marked by continuous refinement and adaptation.

Early Trait Theories:

1. **Great Man Theory (19th Century):**

   - In the 19th century, the Great Man Theory posited that leaders are born, not made. It focused on identifying specific inherent traits that distinguished leaders from non-leaders.
   - Example: Leaders such as Abraham Lincoln and Winston Churchill were often cited as examples of individuals possessing unique qualities that made them exceptional leaders.

2. **Trait Approach (20th Century):**

   - Building on the Great Man Theory, the trait approach sought to identify a definitive set of leadership traits. Researchers aimed to pinpoint the characteristics common to successful leaders.
   - Example: Traits like decisiveness, integrity, and emotional intelligence were considered essential for effective leadership.

Behavioral Theories:

1. **Ohio State Studies (1940s):**

   - The Ohio State Studies marked a shift from trait-focused approaches to behavioral perspectives. Researchers identified two key dimensions of leadership behavior: consideration (relationship-oriented) and initiation of structure (task-oriented).

- Example: Leaders displaying high consideration would prioritize building positive relationships with team members, while those emphasizing initiation of structure would focus on organizing tasks and setting clear expectations.

2. **Michigan Leadership Studies (1950s):**

- The Michigan Leadership Studies expanded on behavioral theories, identifying two leadership styles: employee-oriented and production-oriented. This research emphasized the leader's focus on either the well-being of employees or the accomplishment of tasks.
- Example: A leader adopting an employee-oriented style would prioritize team satisfaction and development, while a production-oriented leader would prioritize task efficiency and achievement.

Contingency Theories:

1. **Fiedler's Contingency Model (1967):**

- Fiedler's model introduced the idea that the effectiveness of a leader is contingent upon the match between their leadership style and the situation. It considered factors such as leader-member relations, task structure, and position power.
- Example: A leader with a task-oriented style may be more effective in situations with clearly defined tasks and strong leader-member relations.

2. **Hersey and Blanchard's Situational Leadership Model (1970s):**

- Hersey and Blanchard's model expanded on contingency theories by considering the maturity level of followers. It proposed that effective leadership involves adapting the leadership style to the readiness of the followers.
- Example: A leader might adopt a more directive style for less mature followers and a more participative style for more mature followers.

Transformational and Transactional Leadership:

1. **Transformational Leadership (1980s):**

- Transformational leadership theory emerged, emphasizing leaders who inspire and motivate followers to achieve beyond their self-interests. It introduced concepts like charisma, vision, and intellectual stimulation.
- Example: Leaders like Nelson Mandela and Martin Luther King Jr. are often cited as transformational leaders who inspired social change through their vision and charisma.

2. **Transactional Leadership Model (1970s-1980s):**

- Transactional leadership theory focused on the exchange between leaders and followers. It included aspects like contingent rewards (rewards for performance) and management-by-exception (intervening only when deviations occur).
- Example: A leader using contingent rewards might offer bonuses or recognition for achieving specific performance goals.

Modern and Inclusive Perspectives:

1. **Servant Leadership (1970s):**

   - Servant leadership shifted the focus from the leader to the followers, emphasizing leaders who prioritize serving others. It incorporates elements of empathy, humility, and a focus on the well-being of followers.
   - Example: CEOs like Howard Schultz of Starbucks are often cited as servant leaders who prioritize the needs of employees and communities.

2. **Authentic Leadership (2000s):**

   - Authentic leadership theory emphasizes leaders who are genuine, self-aware, and true to their values. It encourages leaders to build trust by being transparent and authentic in their actions.
   - Example: Oprah Winfrey is often considered an authentic leader who openly shares her values and experiences.

The evolution of leadership frameworks showcases a progression from trait-focused theories to more dynamic and context-specific models. Modern perspectives emphasize the importance of adaptability, inclusivity, and ethical considerations, reflecting a broader understanding of effective leadership in diverse and ever-changing organizational landscapes.

Criticisms and Limitations of Leadership Frameworks

While leadership frameworks provide valuable insights into understanding and practicing leadership, it's essential to acknowledge their limitations and the criticisms they face. Recognizing these aspects adds nuance to the discussion and helps Leaders' approach leadership frameworks with a balanced perspective.

Overgeneralization:

- **Criticism:** One common critique of leadership frameworks is the tendency to overgeneralize leadership traits or behaviors. Applying a one-size-fits-all approach may oversimplify the complexities of human behavior and individual differences.
- **Limitation Acknowledgement:** Leaders are unique individuals, and effective leadership is influenced by various contextual factors. A trait or behavior that works well in one situation may not be equally effective in another.

Contextual Dynamics:

- **Criticism:** Critics argue that leadership frameworks often fail to adequately consider the situational or cultural context in which leadership occurs. What may be considered effective in one culture or organizational setting might not hold true in another.
- **Limitation Acknowledgement:** Leadership is dynamic, and the effectiveness of specific traits or behaviors can vary based on factors such as culture, industry, and the specific challenges faced by an organization.

Ignoring Fellowship:

- **Criticism:** Some critiques suggest that leadership frameworks often focus too heavily on the leader's characteristics and behaviors, neglecting the important role of followership. Effective leadership is a reciprocal process involving both leaders and followers.
- **Limitation Acknowledgement:** Acknowledge that effective leadership is a collaborative effort. Leaders must consider the needs, expectations, and dynamics of their followers to foster a successful working relationship.

Change Over Time:

- **Criticism:** Leadership is not static; it evolves over time. Some argue that frameworks developed in the past may not adequately address the leadership challenges and dynamics of the present and future.

- **Limitation Acknowledgement:** Leadership frameworks are subject to evolution, and new theories may emerge to address contemporary challenges. Leaders should be open to adapting their approaches based on the changing landscape.

Limited Predictive Power:

- **Criticism:** Critics contend that leadership frameworks may have limited predictive power, meaning they may not reliably forecast leadership success or failure. Leadership is influenced by unpredictable factors that may not be captured by a framework.

- **Limitation Acknowledgement:** While frameworks provide valuable insights, they do not guarantee success. The application of leadership principles is contingent on various unpredictable variables.

Failure to Capture Ethical Dimensions:

- **Criticism:** Some argue that leadership frameworks may not adequately address the ethical dimensions of leadership. Ethical considerations are crucial for effective leadership, and frameworks may not explicitly guide leaders in navigating ethical dilemmas.

- **Limitation Acknowledgement:** Emphasize the importance of ethical leadership and acknowledge that frameworks should be complemented by a strong ethical foundation. Leaders must consider the moral implications of their decisions.

Resistance to Change:

- **Criticism:** Leaders may become entrenched in specific frameworks, resisting the adoption of new ideas or evolving their leadership style. This resistance can hinder adaptability in dynamic environments.

- **Limitation Acknowledgement:** Encourage leaders to remain open to new perspectives and emerging leadership theories. The ability to adapt and embrace change is a crucial aspect of effective leadership.

Leaders to use frameworks as tools, recognizing their strengths while being mindful of their inherent limitations in certain contexts.

Cultural Considerations Leadership Frameworks

Cultural diversity significantly influences how leadership is perceived and practiced. Leadership frameworks may not be universally applied across different cultures, and it's crucial to recognize the impact of cultural nuances on leadership effectiveness.

Cross Cultural Variability:

- **Consideration:** Different cultures have varying expectations regarding leadership behaviors, communication styles, and the exercise of authority. Leaders must be aware of and adapt to these cultural differences to effectively lead diverse teams.

- **Example:** In some cultures, a participative leadership style may be well-received, while in others, a more hierarchical approach might be expected.

Communication Styles:

- **Consideration:** Communication norms vary widely across cultures. Some cultures may value indirect communication, while others may prefer direct and explicit communication. Leaders need to understand and adapt their communication styles accordingly.

- **Example** A leader communicating with a team from a high-context culture may need to pay attention to non-verbal cues and implicit messages.

Power Distance:

- **Consideration:** Power distance, or the extent to which individuals accept hierarchical authority, differs among cultures. Some cultures have a high-power distance, where hierarchical structures are accepted, while others have a low power distance, emphasizing egalitarianism.
- **Example:** In high power distance cultures, leaders may be expected to make decisions autocratically, while in low power distance cultures, participative decision-making may be more valued.

Collectivism vs Individualism:

- **Consideration:** Cultural dimensions such as collectivism (emphasizing group harmony and cooperation) and individualism (emphasizing individual goals and autonomy) impact leadership approaches. Leaders need to understand the collective or individual orientation of their team members.
- **Example:** A leader in a collectivist culture may prioritize team cohesion and harmony, while a leader in an individualist culture may focus on recognizing individual achievements.

Time Orientation:

- **Consideration:** Cultural differences in time orientation, whether past-oriented, present-oriented, or future-oriented, influence how leaders and teams approach deadlines, planning, and goal setting.

- **Example:** A leader working with a team from a future-oriented culture may emphasize long-term planning and goal setting, while a team from a present-oriented culture may prioritize immediate tasks.

Implicit vs Explicit Leadership Expectations:

- **Consideration:** In some cultures, leadership expectations may be implicit and unspoken, requiring leaders to understand subtle cues. In contrast, other cultures may have explicit and clearly defined expectations for leaders.

- **Example:** Leaders working in cultures with explicit expectations may benefit from clearly defined roles and responsibilities, while those in cultures with implicit expectations may need to discern expectations through observation and relationship-building.

Adaptability and Cultural Intelligence:

- **Consideration:** Successful leaders in diverse cultural settings demonstrate cultural intelligence — the ability to adapt and interact effectively across cultures. This adaptability involves a genuine interest in and understanding of different cultural perspectives.

- **Example:** Leaders may undergo cross-cultural training to enhance their cultural intelligence, allowing them to navigate diverse cultural landscapes more effectively.

Balancing Global Consistency and Local Sensitivity:

- **Consideration:** Organizations with a global presence often grapple with the challenge of maintaining consistency in leadership practices while being sensitive to local cultural nuances.

- **Example:** A multinational corporation may establish global leadership values but encourage leaders in different regions to implement these values in ways that align with local cultural norms.

In summary, understanding cultural considerations is paramount for leaders seeking to apply leadership frameworks effectively in diverse settings. By recognizing and adapting to cultural nuances, leaders can foster inclusivity, build strong cross-cultural relationships, and enhance their effectiveness in a globalized world.

Practical Exercises and Reflection Questions

These exercises and reflection questions are designed to encourage readers to actively apply and critically reflect on the concepts discussed in this chapter. They aim to bridge the gap between theory and practical application, fostering a deeper understanding of how leadership frameworks can be valuable tools in real-world leadership scenarios.

1. **Leadership Scenario Analysis:**

   - **Exercise:** Identify a challenging leadership scenario you have faced or anticipate facing. Describe the key elements of the situation, including the context, team dynamics, and challenges.

   - **Reflection Questions:**

     ✓ How would a trait-based leadership framework approach this situation?

     ✓ What behaviors from behavioral leadership theories could be effective in addressing the challenges?

     ✓ Consider the situational factors – which leadership style from a situational framework might be most suitable?

2. **Cross-Cultural Leadership Reflection:**

   Exercise: Reflect on a leadership experience involving a cross-cultural context. Describe the cultural nuances you encountered and how they influenced your leadership approach.

   - **Reflection Questions:**

     ✓ How did cultural considerations impact communication in this scenario?

- ✓ Which cultural dimensions (e.g., power distance, collectivism) played a significant role?
- ✓ What adjustments would you make in your leadership style based on cultural insights?

3. **Leadership Styles Self-Assessment:**

Exercise: Complete a self-assessment of your own leadership style. Consider your preferred traits, behaviors, and decision-making approaches.`

- **Reflection Questions:**

  - ✓ How does your leadership style align with or differ from established frameworks?
  - ✓ Are there areas of your leadership style that you would like to enhance or modify based on leadership theories?

4. **Application to Multiple Frameworks:**

Exercise: Take a leadership challenge you've faced and analyze it from the perspective of two different leadership frameworks. Compare the insights gained from each framework.

- **Reflection Questions:**

  - ✓ How do the two frameworks offer different insights into the same situation?
  - ✓ Are there complementary elements from each framework that could be integrated for a more comprehensive approach?

5. **Development of Personal Leadership Philosophy:**

Exercise: Draft a brief statement outlining your personal leadership philosophy. Consider the values, principles, and approaches that resonate with you.

- **Reflection Questions:**

  ✓ How does your personal philosophy align with or challenge existing leadership frameworks?
  ✓ In what ways can your philosophy be adaptable to different leadership scenarios?

6. **Peer Discussion:**

Exercise: Engage in a discussion with peers or colleagues about a leadership challenge. Share insights, perspectives, and potential solutions based on different leadership frameworks.

- **Reflection Questions:**

  ✓ How did the exchange of ideas contribute to a more comprehensive understanding of the challenge?
  ✓ Were there diverse viewpoints that highlighted the importance of considering multiple frameworks?

Chapter 2

Great Man Theory

As we step back into the corridors of history, the Great Man Theory emerges as a captivating lens through which we understand leadership. Rooted in the 19th century, this theory was not just an intellectual pursuit; it was a paradigm that mirrored the societal structures of its time. Picture an era marked by hierarchical systems, where the belief that leaders were born, not made, echoed through the chambers of power.

Thomas Carlyle, a prominent advocate of the Great Man Theory, envisioned leadership as a destiny bestowed upon an exclusive few. In this historical context, leadership wasn't perceived as a skill to be acquired; rather, it was seen as an inherent trait that set apart those destined for greatness.

The Great Man Theory of Leadership is a traditional concept that suggests that effective leaders possess inherent, natural qualities that distinguish them from others. This theory emerged during the 19th century and was popularized by Scottish historian and essayist Thomas Carlyle. The essence of the Great Man Theory lies in the belief that leadership is not a skill that can be acquired, but rather a set of qualities that are intrinsic to certain individuals.

Key Assumptions of the Great Man Theory

1. **Innate Leadership Qualities:**

    - *Assumption*: Effective leaders are born with innate qualities and traits that set them apart.
    - *Implication*: The theory proposes that leadership cannot be learned or acquired through education or experience; rather, it is a natural endowment.

2. **Leadership is Rare:**

    - *Assumption*: Exceptional leaders are rare and occur sporadically throughout history.
    - *Implication*: The theory suggests that only a select few possess the unique combination of traits that qualify them for leadership roles.

3. **Leaders Emerge in Times of Crisis:**

    - *Assumption*: Great leaders emerge during times of crisis or significant events.
    - *Implication*: The theory implies that the need for leadership arises during critical moments, and individuals with innate leadership qualities naturally step forward.

4. **Uncommon Traits:**

    - *Assumption*: Certain personality traits, such as decisiveness, charisma, and intelligence, are common among great leaders.
    - *Implication*: The theory identifies specific characteristics that are believed to be crucial for effective leadership, emphasizing their rarity.

5. **Irreplaceable Leaders:**

   - *Assumption*: Great leaders are irreplaceable, and their absence results in a leadership void.
   - *Implication*: The theory implies that the impact of great leaders is so profound that finding a suitable replacement is challenging.

6. **Gender Bias:**

   - *Assumption*: Historically, the theory has been biased towards male leaders.
   - *Implication*: The early formulations of the Great Man Theory often excluded or downplayed the leadership potential of women.

7. **Leadership is Situational:**

   - *Assumption*: The effectiveness of leadership is contingent on specific situations.
   - *Implication*: The theory suggests that leaders may not be effective in all circumstances, and their success depends on the context in which they find themselves.

While the Great Man Theory has historical significance, it has been criticized for its lack of empirical evidence, its gender bias, and its oversimplification of the complex nature of leadership. Modern leadership theories often emphasize the importance of learned skills, situational adaptability, and the role of followership in shaping effective leadership.

Real-Life Examples of Great Man Theory of Leadership

The Great Man Theory of Leadership suggests that exceptional leaders possess innate qualities that set them apart, and their impact on history is often irreplaceable. While modern leadership theories may challenge this perspective, historical examples have been often interpreted through the lens of the Great Man Theory. Here are a few historical figures often associated with this theory:

1. **Alexander the Great:**

   - *Innate Qualities*: Charismatic, strategic, and decisive.
   - *Impact*: Alexander's military conquests in the 4th century BCE united vast territories, creating one of the largest empires in history. His innate leadership qualities, including tactical brilliance and the ability to inspire loyalty among his troops, align with the characteristics proposed by the Great Man Theory.

2. **Napolean Bonaparte:**

   - *Innate Qualities*: Charismatic, ambitious, and strategic.
   - *Impact*: Napoleon rose from relative obscurity to become the Emperor of the French in the early 19th century. His military campaigns and political prowess had a profound impact on European history. The theory would argue that Napoleon's innate qualities positioned him as a leader destined for greatness.

3. **Winston Churchill:**

   - *Innate Qualities*: Charismatic, resilient, and eloquent.
   - *Impact*: Churchill's leadership during World War II, particularly his speeches and ability to inspire the British people, is often cited as an example of the Great Man Theory in action. His innate qualities played a crucial role in navigating the challenges of wartime leadership.

4. **Mahatma Gandhi:**

- *Innate Qualities*: Charismatic, principled, and nonviolent.
- *Impact*: Gandhi's leadership during India's struggle for independence in the mid-20th century is seen as an embodiment of the Great Man Theory. His philosophy of nonviolent resistance and ability to mobilize mass movements demonstrated innate qualities that significantly influenced the course of history.

5. **Martin Luther King Jr.:**

- *Innate Qualities*: Charismatic, visionary, and committed to civil rights.
- *Impact*: King's leadership in the American civil rights movement is often viewed through the lens of the Great Man Theory. His ability to articulate a vision of equality and justice, coupled with his charisma and unwavering commitment, made him a transformative leader in the fight against racial discrimination.

What motivates individuals to adopt a Great Man approach to leadership?

The adoption of a Great Man approach to leadership can be motivated by several factors, both internal and external. Here are some key motivators:

1. **Desire for Heroic Leadership:**

- *Motivation*: Some individuals are drawn to the idea of heroic leadership, where a single individual is seen as the saviour or visionary who can lead others to success.
- *Implication*: The desire to be perceived as a heroic figure, capable of making significant impacts on an organization

or society, may drive individuals to embrace the notion that certain leaders are born with exceptional qualities.

2. **Cultural Influences:**

- *Motivation*: Cultural narratives and historical traditions often emphasize the impact of extraordinary leaders. These narratives may highlight the achievements of iconic figures, reinforcing the belief in the innate qualities of great leaders.

- *Implication*: Individuals raised within a cultural context that places a strong emphasis on heroic leadership may be more inclined to adopt a Great Man approach.

3. **Yearning for Certainty and Stability:**

- *Motivation*: The Great Man Theory offers a seemingly clear and deterministic view of leadership. It provides a sense of order and stability, suggesting that effective leaders possess inherent qualities that set them apart.

- *Implication*: In times of uncertainty or change, individuals may be motivated to adopt a Great Man approach as a way to find stability and reassurance in the belief that leaders are predestined.

4. **Attribution of Success to Personal Traits:**

- *Motivation*: People may be inclined to attribute success to the personal traits of leaders rather than considering complex external factors. This simplification can be comforting and may align with a desire for clear cause-and-effect relationships.

- *Implication*: Embracing the Great Man Theory allows individuals to attribute success to the inherent qualities of leaders, making the leadership phenomenon more comprehensible and controllable.

5. **Aspiration of Influence and Recognition:**

   - *Motivation*: Individuals aspiring for leadership roles may be motivated by the belief that possessing certain innate qualities associated with the Great Man Theory will enhance their chances of achieving influence and recognition.
   - *Implication*: The allure of being recognized as a great leader may drive individuals to adopt a perspective that emphasizes the rarity and uniqueness of leadership qualities.

6. **Educational Background and Training:**

   - *Motivation*: Individuals with a traditional education or training in leadership theories may be exposed to historical perspectives like the Great Man Theory. This exposure can shape their beliefs and influence their approach to leadership.
   - *Implication*: Educational experiences that highlight the contributions of exceptional leaders may contribute to the adoption of a Great Man approach.

It's essential to recognize that while the Great Man Theory has historical significance, modern leadership theories emphasize a more nuanced and situational understanding of leadership. The motivations for adopting a Great Man approach may vary, and individuals may find value in exploring alternative perspectives that consider the complexities of leadership in diverse contexts.

Manifestation of Great Man Leadership framework in day-to-day Leadership practices

While the Great Man Theory of Leadership has been criticized and is not the dominant framework in contemporary leadership studies, certain elements of this perspective may still manifest in day-to-day leadership practices. Here are ways in which the Great Man Theory might influence or be reflected in leadership behaviors:

1. **Charismatic Leadership:**

   - *Manifestation*: Leaders exhibiting charismatic qualities, such as a compelling presence, inspirational communication, and an ability to captivate and influence followers.

   - *Implication*: The Great Man Theory emphasizes charisma as one of the inherent qualities of exceptional leaders. In day-to-day practices, a leader's charisma may play a significant role in rallying teams, fostering motivation, and influencing organizational culture.

2. **Visionary Leadership:**

   - *Manifestation*: Leaders who articulate a compelling vision for the future, demonstrating a capacity to inspire and guide others toward a common goal.

   - *Implication*: The notion of visionary leadership aligns with the Great Man Theory's emphasis on leaders possessing a unique ability to envision and shape the future. Day-to-day practices may involve leaders communicating and pursuing a vision that sets them apart.

3. **Decisive Leadership:**

   - *Manifestation*: Leaders making authoritative decisions in a timely manner, displaying confidence and clarity in their choices.

- *Implication*: The Great Man Theory often associates effective leaders with decisiveness. In daily leadership practices, the ability to make quick, informed decisions may be seen as an inherent trait, reflecting the theory's emphasis on leaders born with decision-making capabilities.

4. **Inspirational Communication:**

- *Manifestation*: Leaders employing powerful and motivational communication styles to inspire and influence their teams.
- *Implication*: Effective communication is considered a key quality in the Great Man Theory. Leaders who excel in inspiring others through their words may be perceived as embodying the charismatic and inspirational characteristics associated with this framework.

5. **Uniqueness of Leadership Style:**

- *Manifestation*: Leaders who distinguish themselves through a unique leadership style that stands out within the organization or industry.
- *Implication*: The Great Man Theory suggests that exceptional leaders have distinctive qualities that set them apart. In day-to-day practices, leaders may consciously or unconsciously adopt a unique leadership style, emphasizing their individuality.

6. **Heroic Acts and Impact:**

- *Manifestation*: Leaders who are recognized for their heroic or transformative actions that leave a lasting impact on their teams or organizations.

- *Implication*: The Great Man Theory often attributes historical significance to leaders based on their extraordinary impact. In daily leadership, a focus on achieving remarkable and transformative outcomes may be seen as a reflection of this perspective.

It's important to note that while certain elements of the Great Man Theory may be evident in day-to-day leadership practices, contemporary leadership thinking recognizes the limitations of this perspective. Modern theories emphasize the importance of context, situational factors, and the development of leadership skills over time. Leaders today often strive for a more inclusive and collaborative approach, acknowledging that effective leadership is not solely dependent on inherent traits but can be nurtured and developed through continuous learning and adaptability.

Strategies for cultivating Great Man framework in leadership

Cultivating the Great Man framework in leadership involves recognizing and developing certain traits and behaviors associated with this approach. Here are some strategies for cultivating the Great Man framework:

1. **Self-Reflection and Personal Development:**

   - Encourage leaders to engage in regular self-reflection to gain insight into their strengths, weaknesses, values, and aspirations. This process of introspection allows leaders to understand themselves better and identify areas for growth.
   - Provide opportunities for personal development through workshops, seminars, leadership training programs, and executive coaching sessions. These initiatives can help leaders enhance their self-awareness, emotional

intelligence, communication skills, and leadership competencies.

- Foster a culture of continuous feedback and constructive criticism, encouraging leaders to seek input from peers, mentors, and team members to facilitate their professional growth and development.

2. **Emphasis on Character and Integrity:**

- Instill the importance of character and integrity as foundational principles of leadership. Leaders must uphold ethical standards, honesty, transparency, and accountability in all their interactions and decision-making processes.

- Lead by example, demonstrating integrity, authenticity, and moral courage in their actions and behaviors. When leaders prioritize ethical conduct and demonstrate integrity in their leadership approach, they inspire trust, loyalty, and respect among their team members and stakeholders.

3. **Continuous Learning and Knowledge Acquisition:**

- Foster a culture of continuous learning and knowledge acquisition within the organization, encouraging leaders to stay updated on industry trends, best practices, and emerging technologies relevant to their field.

- Provide access to resources such as books, articles, online courses, webinars, and industry conferences to support leaders' ongoing learning and professional development.

- Create opportunities for leaders to share knowledge, insights, and best practices with their teams and peers, fostering a culture of knowledge sharing and collaboration.

4. **Courage and Resilience:**

- Develop leaders' courage and resilience to navigate challenges, uncertainty, and setbacks effectively. Encourage them to embrace change, take calculated risks, and learn from failures and setbacks.

- Provide opportunities for leaders to develop their problem-solving skills, critical thinking abilities, and decision-making capabilities through real-world experiences, simulations, and case studies.

- Foster a supportive environment where leaders feel empowered to experiment, innovate, and adapt to changing circumstances without fear of failure or repercussion.

5. **Visionary Thinking and Strategic Planning:**

- Foster visionary thinking among leaders by encouraging them to develop a compelling vision for the future of their organization or team. A clear and inspiring vision serves as a guiding beacon, motivating and aligning team members toward common goals and objectives.

- Support leaders in translating their vision into actionable strategies and plans through strategic planning processes. Provide tools, frameworks, and resources to help leaders identify priorities, set goals, allocate resources, and monitor progress toward achieving their vision.

- Encourage leaders to communicate their vision effectively to inspire and engage their teams, fostering a shared sense of purpose, direction, and commitment to organizational success.

6. **Empowerment and Mentorship:**

- Empower leaders to empower others by fostering a culture of mentorship, coaching, and support within the organization. Encourage leaders to mentor and coach aspiring leaders, sharing their knowledge, experiences, and insights to help them grow and develop.

- Provide training and support to help leaders enhance their coaching and mentoring skills, including active listening, constructive feedback, empathy, and empowerment techniques.

- Recognize and reward leaders who demonstrate a commitment to developing and empowering others, fostering a culture of collaboration, growth, and leadership development within the organization.

7. **Recognition and Reward:**

- Recognize and reward leaders who exemplify the traits and behaviors associated with the Great Man framework. Celebrate their achievements, contributions, and positive impact on their teams and organizations through formal recognition programs, awards, and incentives.

- Create a culture of appreciation and gratitude, where leaders feel valued and appreciated for their efforts and contributions. Recognize not only individual accomplishments but also collaborative achievements that demonstrate the collective success of the team or organization.

- Use recognition and reward programs strategically to reinforce desired behaviors and motivate leaders to continue striving for excellence in their leadership roles.

By implementing these strategies, organizations can cultivate the Great Man framework in leadership and foster the development of leaders who inspire, empower, and drive positive change within their teams and organizations.

Great Man Theory: My observation and experience

Amidst the fast-paced world of B2C sales, I had the privilege of witnessing the embodiment of the Great Man Theory in action. This story revolves around Jayant, a remarkable individual whose journey from sales representative to Regional Sales Head – Mumbai at Sterling Holidays Resorts showcased the transformative power of innate leadership qualities.

Jayant's rise to prominence was marked by a unique blend of traits that set him apart from his peers. As he assumed the mantle of Regional Sales Head, his innate qualities began to shine, leaving an indelible mark on the organization.

Jayant's decision-making prowess was evident from the outset, a product of years spent navigating the intricacies of the sales landscape. When confronted with critical choices that could shape the company's sales trajectory, his clarity of vision and unwavering confidence guided us through the challenges.

However, it was not just Jayant's strategic acumen that distinguished him. His charisma was magnetic, drawing colleagues and clients alike to his orbit. Whether leading high-stakes negotiations or motivating the sales team, Jayant's presence was a catalyst for success, instilling confidence, and inspiring excellence.

Yet, perhaps Jayant's most remarkable quality was his resilience in the face of adversity. In moments of uncertainty and setback, he remained steadfast, a pillar of strength for his team. His unwavering commitment to driving sales growth fueled his determination to overcome obstacles and emerge stronger than before. No wonder, Mumbai region used to lead the entire country by leaps and bounds in Vacation Ownership sales at Sterling Holidays Resorts.

Reflecting on Jayant's journey, I am reminded of the profound impact that inherent leadership qualities can have on organizational success. His story serves as a testament to the enduring relevance of the Great Man Theory, highlighting the transformative potential of individuals who possess innate leadership traits.

As we navigate the complexities of corporate leadership, let us draw inspiration from Jayant's example. Let us recognize the significance of inherent qualities in shaping leadership effectiveness and strive to cultivate these traits within ourselves and our teams. In doing so, we can chart a course toward organizational excellence, guided by the timeless principles of the Great Man Theory.

Conclusion

In the annals of leadership theories, the Great Man Theory has left an indelible mark, shaping our understanding of leadership for generations. Its assertion that exceptional leaders are born with innate qualities has sparked both admiration and skepticism. As we delve into the realms of history, we encounter charismatic figures whose impact seems almost predestined, giving credence to the theory's perspective.

However, the contemporary landscape of leadership thought has evolved, acknowledging the limitations of the Great Man Theory. While charisma, vision, and decisiveness undoubtedly play crucial roles in leadership, modern theories emphasize a more nuanced and context-dependent approach. Leadership, it seems, is not a fixed mantle bestowed upon a select few, but a dynamic interplay of skills, adaptability, and the ability to connect with and inspire others.

In reflecting upon the Great Man Theory, I find myself drawn to the idea that leadership is a tapestry woven from both innate qualities and the threads of experience. While certain individuals possess remarkable inherent traits, the journey of leadership is one of continuous learning, growth, and adaptation. True leadership, in my view, embraces a diversity of approaches, recognizing that effective leaders can emerge from unexpected quarters.

As we bid farewell to the Great Man Theory, let us carry forward its lessons in humility, acknowledging the potential for leadership to emerge from the unlikeliest of sources. The future of leadership lies in a mosaic that embraces diverse qualities, continuously evolving and adapting to the complexities of the world we navigate together.

Practical Exercises and Reflection Questions

These exercises and reflection questions are designed to encourage readers to actively apply and critically reflect on the concepts discussed in this chapter. They aim to bridge the gap between theory and practical application, fostering a deeper understanding of how leadership frameworks can be valuable tools in real-world leadership scenarios.

1. **Leadership Trait Analysis:**

   - Identify three leaders you admire and list the traits you believe make them effective.
   - Reflect on whether these traits align with the characteristics proposed by the Great Man Theory.
   - Consider how these leaders' innate qualities contribute to their impact.

2. **Personal Leadership Traits:**

   - Conduct a self-assessment of your own leadership traits and qualities.
   - Identify areas where you believe you naturally excel as a leader.
   - Explore how these traits align or differ from the characteristics associated with the Great Man Theory.

3. **Historical Case Study:**

   - Choose a historical figure recognized as a great leader.
   - Analyze their life and leadership style through the lens of the Great Man Theory.
   - Reflect on how their innate qualities contributed to their historical impact.

Reflection Questions

1. **In your Leadership Journey:**

   - Have you ever encountered a leader whom you felt embodied the characteristics of the Great Man Theory?
   - How did their innate qualities contribute to their effectiveness as a leader?
   - Reflect on any instances where you felt your own innate traits played a significant role in your leadership.

2. **Nature vs Nurture:**

   - Do you believe that effective leadership is primarily a result of inherent traits, or do learnt skills and experiences play a more significant role?
   - Consider how your beliefs about leadership origins influence your approach to personal and professional development.

3. **Applicability in your context:**

   - In your current leadership role, do you feel that certain innate qualities are more valued or necessary for success?
   - How might the Great Man Theory apply or diverge from the leadership expectations in your specific organizational or cultural context?

4. **Leadership Challenges:**

   - Reflect on a challenging leadership situation you've encountered.

- Consider how the application of innate leadership qualities, as proposed by the Great Man Theory, might have influenced the outcome.
- Explore alternative approaches that could have been effective in the given context.

5. **Developmental Opportunities:**

- Identify one leadership trait or quality you would like to further develop.
- Outline specific actions or learning opportunities you can undertake to enhance this aspect of your leadership.
- Consider how intentional development aligns with or challenges the concept of innate leadership traits.

Chapter 3

Trait Theory

In the vast landscape of leadership theories, few have captured the imagination and sparked as much debate as Trait Theory. At its core, Trait Theory proposes that effective leaders possess inherent qualities that set them apart from others. These traits, it suggests, are not acquired through experience or education but are ingrained within individuals from birth.

As we embark on our exploration of Trait Theory in this chapter, we are compelled to consider the profound implications of this perspective. At its essence, Trait Theory challenges us to confront the age-old question: Are leaders born or made?

Through the lens of Trait Theory, we peer into the inner workings of leadership, seeking to unravel the mysteries that lie beneath the surface. Here, we are invited to delve beyond the surface-level behaviors and situational dynamics to uncover the fundamental traits that define leadership effectiveness.

Trait Theory posits that certain characteristics—such as intelligence, self-confidence, integrity, decisiveness, emotional stability, and sociability—serve as the building blocks of effective leadership. These traits are believed to be relatively stable over time and across various contexts, shaping an individual's leadership style and approach.

Yet, as we delve deeper into the realm of Trait Theory, we are confronted with a myriad of questions and complexities. Can leadership truly be distilled into a set of innate qualities, or are there situational factors and learned behaviors that also contribute to leadership effectiveness? How do we reconcile the notion of trait-based leadership with the dynamic and ever-evolving nature of organizational environments?

In our quest for answers, we turn to both theoretical frameworks and real-world examples, seeking to uncover the truths that lie at the intersection of theory and practice. Through a careful examination of the research literature and insights gleaned from personal experiences, we aim to shed light on the relevance and implications of Trait Theory in contemporary leadership contexts.

As we journey through this chapter, we invite readers to embark on a voyage of discovery—a journey that will challenge preconceived notions, provoke critical thinking, and perhaps even reshape our understanding of what it means to be an effective leader. Together, let us unravel the mysteries of Trait Theory and unlock the secrets of leadership excellence.

Definition and Key Concepts of Trait Theory

Trait Theory of Leadership is a framework that focuses on the innate characteristics or traits possessed by individuals that predispose them to leadership roles. Here are the key concepts of Trait Theory elaborated:

1. **Innate Qualities:**

   Trait Theory posits that certain traits are inherent to individuals and contribute to their effectiveness as leaders. These traits are believed to be relatively stable over time and across different situations, forming the foundation of an individual's leadership style and approach.

2. **Identified Leadership Traits:**

   Trait Theory identifies specific traits associated with effective leadership. Commonly cited traits include intelligence, self-confidence, integrity, decisiveness, emotional stability, sociability, and resilience. These traits are believed to distinguish effective leaders from others and play a crucial role in determining leadership effectiveness.

3. **Trait-based Leadership Assessment:**

   Trait Theory suggests that leadership potential can be assessed based on an individual's possession of specific traits. Assessment tools such as personality assessments, behavioral interviews, and competency evaluations are often used to identify and measure these traits in individuals aspiring to leadership roles.

4. **Trait Stability:**

   One of the foundational principles of Trait Theory is the stability of leadership traits. It suggests that these traits remain relatively consistent over time and are resistant to change, regardless of situational factors or external influences. This stability implies that individuals possess inherent qualities that predispose them to leadership roles from an early age.

5. **Trait-based Leadership Development:**

   Trait Theory acknowledges the potential for leadership development but emphasizes that it is primarily focused on refining and enhancing existing traits rather than fundamentally altering them. Leadership development initiatives may include self-awareness exercises, feedback mechanisms, coaching, and mentoring aimed at leveraging and optimizing individuals' inherent traits.

6. **Trait Interaction:**

Trait Theory acknowledges that leadership effectiveness is not solely determined by the presence of individual traits but also by the interaction and combination of multiple traits. Effective leaders often exhibit a balance of various traits, depending on the demands of specific situations and contexts. Understanding how different traits interact and complement each other is essential for effective leadership practice.

7. **Trait Contingency:**

While Trait Theory emphasizes the importance of innate qualities in leadership effectiveness, it also recognizes the role of situational factors and environmental contexts. Trait contingency suggests that certain traits may be more advantageous in specific situations or organizational contexts. Effective leaders adapt their behavior and leverage their traits accordingly to navigate diverse challenges and opportunities.

8. **Critiques and Limitations:**

Despite its historical significance, Trait Theory has faced critiques and limitations. Critics argue that Trait Theory oversimplifies the complexities of leadership by focusing solely on individual traits and neglecting situational factors, social dynamics, and contextual influences. Additionally, the lack of consensus on universally applicable leadership traits and the challenge of accurately measuring and assessing traits pose significant limitations to the practical application of Trait Theory.

In summary, Trait Theory of Leadership offers valuable insights into the inherent qualities that contribute to leadership effectiveness. By understanding and leveraging these key concepts, individuals and organizations can gain a deeper understanding of leadership potential and cultivate effective leadership practices.

Impact of Traits on Leadership: Shaping Leadership Effectiveness

Understanding the intricate relationship between leadership traits and effectiveness is essential for comprehending the nuances of Trait Theory. Let's delve deeper into how these traits exert their influence on leadership and organizational outcomes:

1. **Influence on Leadership Style:**

   Leadership traits serve as the bedrock upon which individuals develop their unique leadership styles. Traits such as intelligence, confidence, integrity, decisiveness, emotional stability, and sociability profoundly influence how leaders interact with their teams, make decisions, and navigate challenges.

   - ***Intelligence:*** Leaders with high levels of intelligence often demonstrate strategic thinking, problem-solving abilities, and a capacity to grasp complex concepts. Their intellectual prowess enables them to analyze situations critically, anticipate trends, and make informed decisions that propel the organization forward.

   - ***Confidence:*** Confidence is a hallmark trait of effective leaders, instilling trust and inspiring followership. Confident leaders exude assurance in their abilities and decisions, fostering a sense of stability and direction within their teams.

- **_Integrity:_** Leaders who prioritize integrity uphold ethical standards and moral principles in their actions and decisions. Their commitment to honesty, transparency, and fairness fosters a culture of trust and accountability, laying the foundation for strong interpersonal relationships and organizational cohesion.

- **_Decisiveness:_** Decisive leaders possess the ability to make timely and effective decisions, even in the face of uncertainty or ambiguity. Their clarity of thought and action instills confidence in their teams, driving momentum and progress towards organizational goals.

- **_Emotional Stability:_** Leaders with emotional stability demonstrate resilience in the face of adversity and maintain composure under pressure. Their ability to manage their emotions and navigate challenging situations with grace and poise inspires confidence and reassures their teams.

- **_Sociability:_** Sociable leaders excel in interpersonal relationships and communication, fostering open dialogue, collaboration, and teamwork within their organizations. Their approachable demeanor and empathetic nature create a supportive work environment where individuals feel valued and heard.

By understanding how these traits shape leadership styles, we gain insights into the diverse ways in which leaders lead and influence their organizational contexts.

2. **Examples of Trait-Driven Leadership:**

Real-life examples vividly illustrate how specific leadership traits can drive success or present challenges within organizations. Consider the case of Steve Jobs, whose visionary leadership and relentless pursuit of innovation revolutionized the tech industry. Jobs' unwavering self-confidence, creativity, and decisiveness enabled him to lead Apple to unprecedented heights, despite facing numerous obstacles along the way.

Conversely, the downfall of Enron under the leadership of Jeffrey Skilling serves as a cautionary tale of leadership traits gone awry. Skilling's intelligence and charisma were overshadowed by a lack of integrity and ethical misconduct, ultimately leading to the company's demise and a tarnished legacy.

These examples highlight how leadership traits, when harnessed effectively, can drive organizational success, but when mismanaged or neglected, can lead to significant challenges and setbacks.

3. **Impact on Organizational Outcomes:**

Leadership traits have a profound impact on organizational outcomes, shaping employee engagement, team performance, and overall organizational culture. Leaders who embody positive traits such as integrity, empathy, and decisiveness often cultivate a supportive and inclusive work environment where individuals feel motivated, empowered, and valued.

Conversely, leaders who exhibit negative traits such as arrogance, impulsivity, or dishonesty may undermine trust, erode morale, and foster a toxic organizational culture characterized by fear, resentment, and disengagement.

Research indicates that leadership traits significantly influence employee satisfaction, retention rates, productivity levels, and ultimately, organizational success. By fostering a culture of trust, accountability, and collaboration, leaders can harness the power of positive traits to drive high-performance teams and achieve strategic objectives.

In summary, the impact of leadership traits on effectiveness is multifaceted, influencing not only individual leadership styles but also organizational dynamics and outcomes. By understanding the interplay between traits and leadership effectiveness, organizations can cultivate strong, resilient leadership that fosters a culture of growth, innovation, and success.

What motivates individuals to adopt Trait Theory approach to leadership?

Several factors can motivate individuals to adopt a Trait Theory approach to leadership:

- ***Belief in Inherent Qualities***: Individuals who subscribe to Trait Theory often believe that effective leaders possess innate qualities that predispose them to leadership roles. This belief stems from the notion that certain traits, such as intelligence, confidence, and integrity, are inherent and relatively stable over time. Those who hold this belief may be motivated to adopt a Trait Theory approach as it aligns with their understanding of leadership effectiveness.

- ***Desire for Clarity and Predictability***: Trait Theory provides a structured framework for understanding leadership by focusing on specific traits and their impact on leadership effectiveness. For individuals who seek clarity and predictability in their leadership approach, Trait Theory offers a clear roadmap for identifying and developing key leadership traits. By focusing on innate qualities, individuals may feel more confident in their ability to assess and cultivate their leadership capabilities.

- ***Aspiration for Personal Development***: Adopting a Trait Theory approach can be motivated by a desire for personal growth and development. Individuals may see Trait Theory to identify their strengths and areas for improvement as leaders. By understanding which traits are associated with effective leadership, individuals can focus their efforts on developing those traits through self-awareness, learning, and practice.

- ***Validation of Leadership Potential***: For individuals who possess traits commonly associated with effective leadership, adopting a Trait Theory approach can serve as validation of their leadership potential. Recognizing that their innate qualities align with those identified in Trait Theory may bolster their confidence and encourage them to pursue leadership roles with greater conviction.

- ***Seeking Role Models***: Trait Theory often highlights historical or contemporary leaders who exemplify the traits associated with effective leadership. Individuals may be motivated to adopt a Trait Theory approach as they aspire to emulate the leadership qualities demonstrated by these role models. By studying and learning from the successes and challenges of leaders with similar traits, individuals can gain insights into effective leadership practices.

- ***Organizational Expectations***: In some cases, organizational cultures or contexts may emphasize Trait Theory as a preferred approach to leadership. Leaders may be encouraged or expected to demonstrate specific traits that align with the organization's values, goals, or cultural norms. In such environments, individuals may adopt a Trait Theory approach to leadership as a means of meeting these expectations and effectively leading within the organization.

Overall, individuals may be motivated to adopt a Trait Theory approach to leadership for various reasons, including their beliefs about inherent qualities, desire for clarity and predictability, aspiration for personal development, validation of leadership potential, seeking role models, and alignment with organizational expectations.

Manifestation of Trait Theory of Leadership framework in day-to-day Leadership practices

The manifestation of Trait Theory in day-to-day leadership practices can be observed across various dimensions of leadership behavior and interactions. Here's how the framework influences leadership practices in practical scenarios:

- **Trait-based Decision Making:** Leaders who adhere to Trait Theory often rely on their innate characteristics when making decisions. For example, a leader with a high level of decisiveness may be inclined to make swift and confident decisions based on their intuition and judgment. Similarly, a leader with strong emotional stability may approach decision-making calmly and rationally, even in high-pressure situations.

- **Communication and Influence**: Leadership traits such as charisma, confidence, and sociability play a significant role in communication and influence. Leaders who possess these traits may excel in inspiring and motivating their teams, communicating vision and goals effectively, and gaining buy-in from stakeholders. Their ability to connect with others on a personal level enhances their influence and fosters trust and collaboration.

- **Team Dynamics and Collaboration**: Trait Theory emphasizes the importance of traits such as empathy, integrity, and openness in fostering positive team dynamics and collaboration. Leaders who prioritize these traits create a supportive and inclusive work environment where team members feel valued, respected, and motivated to contribute their best efforts. Such leaders encourage open communication, actively listen to team members' perspectives, and promote a culture of trust and mutual respect.

- **Conflict Resolution and Problem Solving**: Leadership traits such as emotional intelligence, resilience, and adaptability are instrumental in navigating conflicts and solving problems effectively. Leaders who possess these traits demonstrate empathy and understanding in resolving interpersonal conflicts, mediating disputes, and finding mutually beneficial solutions. Their ability to remain composed and flexible in the face of challenges enables them to overcome obstacles and drive progress.

- **Leading by Example**: Trait Theory underscores the importance of leaders setting a positive example through their actions and behaviors. Leaders who embody the traits associated with effective leadership serve as role models for their teams, inspiring others to emulate their professionalism, integrity, and work ethic. By consistently demonstrating these traits in their day-to-day actions, leaders reinforce organizational values and foster a culture of excellence.

- **Continuous Self-Reflection and Development**: Leaders who adhere to Trait Theory engage in continuous self-reflection and development to enhance their leadership effectiveness. They recognize that leadership traits are not static but can be cultivated and refined over time through self-awareness, learning, and practice. By actively seeking feedback, seeking opportunities for growth, and refining their leadership skills, these leaders strive to become more effective and impactful in their roles.

In summary, Trait Theory influences day-to-day leadership practices by guiding decision-making, communication, team dynamics, conflict resolution, leading by example, and fostering continuous self-reflection and development. Leaders who embrace this framework leverage their innate characteristics to inspire, motivate, and empower their teams, driving organizational success and growth.

Reconciliation of Trait based Leadership with the Organizational environment.

Reconciling the notion of trait-based leadership with the dynamic and ever-evolving nature of organizational environments requires a nuanced approach that acknowledges both the enduring significance of leadership traits and the need for adaptability and flexibility in response to changing contexts. Here's how this reconciliation can be achieved:

- **Trait Adaptability**: While leadership traits are believed to be relatively stable over time, effective leaders must possess the ability to adapt and flexibly apply their traits to suit evolving organizational environments. This involves recognizing that different situations may require different leadership approaches and being willing to adjust one's behavior and decision-making style accordingly.

- **Trait Development**: Trait-based leadership does not preclude the possibility of trait development or enhancement. Even though individuals may possess inherent leadership traits, there is still room for growth and refinement through deliberate practice, feedback, and learning experiences. Leaders should actively seek opportunities for self-improvement and invest in their personal and professional development to stay relevant in dynamic organizational environments.

- **Situational Leadership**: Trait-based leadership can be complemented by the principles of situational leadership, which emphasize the importance of adapting leadership styles to fit the specific needs of the situation or context. Effective leaders recognize that no single leadership style or set of traits is universally applicable and instead tailor their approach based on the demands of the situation, the characteristics of the team, and the organizational culture.

- **Trait Complementarity**: Rather than viewing trait-based leadership and situational leadership as mutually exclusive, leaders can integrate these approaches to leverage the strengths of both frameworks. By understanding how different traits interact and complement each other, leaders can develop a more holistic and adaptive leadership style that is better suited to the complexities of modern organizational environments.

- **Continuous Learning and Adaptation**: In dynamic organizational environments, leaders must embrace a mindset of continuous learning and adaptation. This involves remaining open to new ideas, perspectives, and approaches, as well as actively seeking feedback and staying informed about changes in the external landscape. By cultivating a learning orientation, leaders can stay agile and responsive in the face of evolving challenges and opportunities.

- **Balancing Stability and Agility**: Reconciling trait-based leadership with the dynamic nature of organizational environments requires striking a balance between stability and agility. While certain leadership traits provide a stable foundation for leadership effectiveness, leaders must also be willing to challenge conventional wisdom, experiment with new approaches, and adapt to changing circumstances to remain effective in an ever-evolving landscape.

In essence, reconciling trait-based leadership with the dynamic nature of organizational environments involves embracing both stability and adaptability, recognizing the enduring significance of leadership traits while remaining flexible and responsive to the evolving needs and challenges of the organization. By integrating trait-based principles with situational awareness and continuous learning, leaders can navigate complex organizational environments with confidence and effectiveness.

Real Life Examples Illustrating Leaders who Exemplify Trait-based Leadership

Examining real-life leaders can provide concrete examples of how Trait Theory manifests in practice. These examples provide tangible illustrations of how specific traits can manifest in the behaviors and decisions of influential leaders. Readers can use these cases to deepen their understanding of Trait Theory by seeing how these traits are applied in real-world leadership scenarios.

Oprah Winfrey

Traits Highlighted: Charisma, Empathy, Resilience

Application: Oprah Winfrey, a media mogul, and philanthropist, exemplifies several traits associated with effective leadership. Her charisma is evident in her ability to connect with audiences, creating a sense of trust and authenticity. Oprah's empathetic communication style, demonstrated through her talk show and interviews, reflects the importance of understanding and relating to others—an essential trait for effective leaders. Additionally, her resilience in overcoming personal challenges and building a successful media empire underscores the enduring nature of certain leadership traits.

Warren Buffett

Traits Highlighted: Judicious Decision-Making, Vision, Humility

Application: Warren Buffett, the renowned investor and CEO of Berkshire Hathaway, showcases traits that align with effective leadership. His judicious decision-making, especially in the realm of value investing, highlights the importance of sound judgment and strategic thinking for leaders. Buffett's long-term vision, evident in his investment philosophy, reflects the trait of foresight and goal orientation. Moreover, his humility and down-to-earth communication style underscores the significance of approachability and humility in effective leadership.

Angela Merkel

Traits Highlighted: Resilience, Decisiveness, Integrity

Application: Angela Merkel, the former Chancellor of Germany, demonstrates leadership traits that have contributed to her political success. Her resilience is evident in navigating complex political landscapes and addressing challenges such as the European financial crisis and the refugee crisis. Merkel's decisiveness, especially in times of crisis, highlights the trait of making tough decisions for the greater good. Furthermore, her reputation for integrity underscores the importance of honesty and ethical conduct in leadership.

Strategies for cultivating Trait Theory framework in leadership

Cultivating the Trait Theory framework in leadership involves focusing on developing and enhancing specific traits and characteristics associated with effective leadership. Here are strategies for cultivating the Trait Theory framework in leadership:

1. **Assessment and Self-Awareness:**

   - Encourage leaders to undergo personality assessments, such as the Myers-Briggs Type Indicator (MBTI) or the Big Five personality traits, to gain insight into their natural tendencies, strengths, and areas for development.

   - Promote self-awareness by encouraging leaders to reflect on their own behaviors, attitudes, and emotional intelligence. Provide opportunities for leaders to receive feedback from peers, mentors, and direct reports to gain a deeper understanding of their leadership style and its impact on others.

2. **Continuous Learning and Development:**

   - Provide leadership development programs and training sessions focused on enhancing specific traits associated with effective leadership, such as communication skills, empathy, resilience, and adaptability.

- Offer workshops, seminars, and coaching sessions to help leaders develop and refine their emotional intelligence, self-management, and interpersonal skills. Provide resources and tools to support ongoing learning and development efforts.

3. **Role Modeling and Mentorship:**

- Encourage leaders to seek out mentorship and guidance from more experienced leaders who exemplify the traits and behaviors associated with effective leadership. Pair leaders with mentors who can provide valuable insights, advice, and support as they work to develop their leadership capabilities.

- Foster a culture of peer-to-peer learning and support, where leaders can observe and learn from the behaviors of their colleagues who demonstrate strong leadership traits. Encourage leaders to emulate positive role models and incorporate their best practices into their own leadership approach.

4. **Feedback and Reflection:**

- Establish a culture of feedback and reflection where leaders regularly solicit input from their peers, direct reports, and supervisors on their leadership effectiveness. Provide opportunities for leaders to receive 360-degree feedback assessments to gain comprehensive insights into their strengths and areas for improvement.

- Encourage leaders to engage in reflective practices, such as journaling or regular self-assessment exercises, to track their progress, identify patterns of behavior, and set goals for continued growth and development.

5. **Skill Building and Practice:**

- Offer skill-building workshops and experiential learning opportunities to help leaders develop specific leadership competencies associated with trait-based leadership, such as decision-making, conflict resolution, team building, and problem-solving.

- Provide opportunities for leaders to practice and apply their newly acquired skills in real-world scenarios through role-playing exercises, case studies, and leadership simulations. Offer constructive feedback and coaching to help leaders refine their abilities and build confidence in their leadership capabilities.

6. **Promotion and Recognition:**

- Recognize and reward leaders who demonstrate the traits and behaviors associated with effective leadership. Celebrate examples of leadership excellence and highlight individuals who embody the organization's core values and leadership principles.

- Provide opportunities for leaders to showcase their leadership abilities through special projects, cross-functional initiatives, or leadership development programs. Offer promotional opportunities and career advancement paths for leaders who consistently demonstrate strong leadership traits and make significant contributions to the organization.

By implementing these strategies, organizations can effectively cultivate the Trait Theory framework in leadership, enabling leaders to develop and leverage their innate qualities to inspire, motivate, and lead others effectively.

Trait Theory: My observation and experience

In the dynamic realm of corporate leadership, the principles of Trait Theory often manifest themselves in subtle yet impactful ways. Allow me to share a story from my own experiences that illustrates the essence of Trait Theory in action.

As a young manager in a multinational corporation at the BBC, I had the privilege of working closely with a senior executive, Seema Mohapatra. Seema possessed a remarkable blend of traits that set her apart as a leader within the organization.

One instance stands out vividly in my memory. Our team was facing a critical decision regarding the launch of a new product line, and tensions were running high. As discussions grew heated and opinions clashed, Seema stepped in to lead the deliberations.

What struck me most about Seema was her unwavering confidence and decisiveness. Despite the complexity of the situation, she exuded a calm assurance that instantly put the team at ease. Her clarity of vision and ability to articulate a clear path forward instilled confidence and inspired trust among team members.

Moreover, Seema's emotional intelligence was evident in her approach to communication and conflict resolution. She took the time to actively listen to each team member's perspective, acknowledging their concerns and validating their contributions. Her empathy and understanding created a safe space for open dialogue and constructive debate, fostering collaboration and creativity within the team.

Throughout the decision-making process, Seema consistently demonstrated integrity and professionalism, leading by example and upholding the organization's values. Her commitment to transparency and fairness instilled a sense of trust and credibility, garnering respect and admiration from colleagues at all levels of the organization.

In reflecting on Seema's leadership style, it became apparent to me how her innate traits aligned with the principles of Trait Theory. Her intelligence, confidence, emotional stability, empathy, and integrity were not merely attributes she possessed but integral components of her leadership identity.

Through Seema's example, I gained a deeper appreciation for the relevance and impact of Trait Theory in corporate leadership. Her ability to leverage her inherent qualities to inspire, motivate, and guide our team toward success was a testament to the enduring validity of this framework.

As I continue to navigate my own leadership journey, I draw inspiration from Seema's example, striving to cultivate and embody the traits associated with effective leadership. In doing so, I remain steadfast in my commitment to driving organizational excellence and fostering a culture of growth, innovation, and collaboration.

In the ever-evolving landscape of corporate leadership, Trait Theory serves as a timeless guide, illuminating the path toward effective leadership and organizational success. Through observation, reflection, and practice, we can harness the power of our innate qualities to become the leaders our teams and organizations need us to be.

Conclusion

As we draw to a close on our exploration of Trait Theory in leadership, I am reminded of the intricate dance between inherent qualities and the ever-shifting landscape of organizational environments. Trait Theory offers a compelling framework through which we can understand the enduring qualities that underpin effective leadership. Yet, it is equally important to acknowledge the dynamic nature of leadership and the need for adaptability in the face of change.

Throughout this chapter, we have delved into the foundational principles of Trait Theory, examining the significance of innate characteristics such as intelligence, confidence, integrity, and empathy in shaping leadership effectiveness. We have explored how these traits manifest in day-to-day leadership practices, influencing decision-making, communication, team dynamics, and organizational outcomes.

However, as leaders, we must recognize that leadership is not a static concept confined to a set of predetermined traits. Rather, it is a dynamic and multifaceted phenomenon that evolves in response to shifting contexts, emerging challenges, and new opportunities. While Trait Theory provides valuable insights into the qualities associated with effective leadership, it is essential to complement this framework with a willingness to adapt, learn, and grow.

My own journey has been enriched by the principles of Trait Theory, as I have witnessed firsthand the impact of inherent qualities on leadership effectiveness. Yet, I have also come to appreciate the importance of remaining agile and responsive in the face of organizational change. As leaders, we must strive to strike a balance between stability and adaptability, leveraging our innate traits while embracing new perspectives and approaches to leadership.

In closing, let us continue to draw inspiration from the timeless wisdom of Trait Theory while remaining open to the possibilities of growth, innovation, and transformation. By embracing both the enduring qualities that define us and the ever-evolving nature of leadership, we can navigate the complexities of organizational environments with grace, resilience, and effectiveness.

As we embark on the next chapter of our leadership journey, may we carry with us the lessons learned from Trait Theory and the conviction that, with courage, curiosity, and compassion, we can lead with purpose and impact in an ever-changing world.

Practical Exercises and Reflection Questions

These exercises and reflection questions are designed to encourage readers to actively apply and critically reflect on the concepts discussed in this chapter. They aim to bridge the gap between theory and practical application, fostering a deeper understanding of how leadership frameworks can be valuable tools in real-world leadership scenarios.

1. **Self-reflection on Leadership Traits:**

   - **Exercise:** Identify three leadership traits that you believe are essential for effective leadership based on your understanding of Trait Theory.

   - **Reflection Questions:**

     - ✓ How have these traits manifested in your past leadership experiences?
     - ✓ Are there specific situations where you felt certain traits were more crucial than others?
     - ✓ In what ways can you further develop or leverage these traits in your current or future leadership roles?

2. **Trait-based Leadership Assessment:**

   - **Exercise:** Take a trait-based leadership assessment, if available, to identify your perceived strengths and areas for growth in relation to key leadership traits.

   - **Reflection Questions:**

     - ✓ Were the results consistent with your self-perception of your leadership traits?
     - ✓ How might the identified traits contribute to or hinder your effectiveness as a leader?
     - ✓ What actions can you take to enhance traits that are crucial for effective leadership?

3. **Traits in Challenging Leadership Scenarios:**

- **Exercise:** Reflect on a challenging leadership scenario you've encountered and analyze which traits, as per Trait Theory, would have been most valuable in that situation.
- **Reflection Questions:**

  ✓ Were there specific traits that, if emphasized, could have positively influenced the outcome?
  ✓ How did your own leadership traits come into play during the challenging scenario?
  ✓ What adjustments, if any, would you make in handling a similar situation in the future based on trait-based insights?

4. **Traits and Team Dynamics:**

- **Exercise:** Consider the dynamics of a team you lead or have been a part of. Identify the leadership traits that have positively influenced team collaboration and performance.
- **Reflection Questions:**

  ✓ Which traits have contributed to fostering a positive team environment?
  ✓ Have there been instances where certain traits were particularly relevant in managing team dynamics?
  ✓ How can an awareness of trait-based leadership enhance your ability to lead and collaborate within a team?

5. **Traits in Leadership Role Models:**

- **Exercise:** Identify a leader you admire and analyze the traits that make them effective. Consider how their traits align with or deviate from traditional Trait Theory.

- **Reflection Questions:**

  - ✓ What specific traits do you believe contribute to this leader's success?
  - ✓ Are there traits they exhibit that challenge conventional notions of effective leadership?
  - ✓ How can insights from their traits inform your own leadership approach?

6. **Developmental Action Plan:**

   - **Exercise:** Develop a personal action plan for further developing specific leadership traits based on your reflections and assessments.
   - **Reflection Questions:**

     - ✓ Which traits do you believe require further development for your growth as a leader?
     - ✓ What specific actions can you take to enhance these traits over the next month, quarter, or year?
     - ✓ How will you measure progress and success in cultivating these traits?

Chapter 4

Behavioral Theories

As we navigate the intricate terrain of leadership theory, Behavioral Theories emerge as guiding beacons, illuminating the tangible actions and behaviors that shape effective leadership. For me, this chapter holds a special significance, as it marks a profound exploration into the heart of leadership dynamics—one that resonates deeply with my own experiences and observations.

Throughout my career journey, I've been privileged to witness firsthand the transformative power of leadership behaviors in driving organizational success. From the inspiring guidance of mentors to the collaborative spirit of high-performing teams, the essence of effective leadership has always been palpable in the behaviors exhibited by individuals at all levels of the organization.

Behavioral Theories offer a compelling framework through which we can dissect and analyze these observable actions, unraveling the intricacies of leadership effectiveness. By studying the behaviors of leaders in diverse contexts and situations, we gain valuable insights into the underlying principles that govern their actions and decisions.

In this chapter, we embark on a voyage of discovery—a journey that transcends mere theoretical frameworks to delve into the lived experiences and practical realities of leadership in action. Through a careful examination of behavioral principles, case studies, and personal anecdotes, we aim to uncover the essence of leadership behaviors and their profound impact on organizational outcomes.

As we delve deeper into the realm of Behavioral Theories, I invite you to join me in reflecting on your own experiences and observations of leadership behaviors. Together, let us explore the intricate tapestry of actions and behaviors that define effective leadership, seeking to glean lessons and insights that will inform and enrich our own leadership journeys.

In the pages that follow, we will unravel the essence of leadership actions, exploring the fundamental principles that underpin Behavioral Theories and their relevance in contemporary organizational contexts. Through this exploration, may we deepen our understanding of the dynamic interplay between behaviors and leadership effectiveness, paving the way for growth, inspiration, and impact in our leadership endeavors.

Behavioral Theories of leadership shift the focus from inherent traits to observable behaviors, emphasizing that effective leadership is a result of actions and interactions. This chapter explores the foundation of Behavioral Theories, analyzes key behaviors, and styles, and presents case studies that highlight leaders embodying different behavioral approaches.

Explanation of Behavioral Theories in Leadership

Core Tenet

Behavioral Theories of leadership represent a departure from earlier trait-based perspectives, shifting the focus from inherent characteristics to observable actions and behaviors. The core tenet asserts that effective leadership is not solely determined by traits one is born with but is, instead, shaped by how individuals behave and interact with others in their leadership roles. This perspective suggests that leadership is a set of learned behaviors that can be developed and refined over time.

Key Points

Observable Behaviors: Leadership, according to Behavioral Theories, is about what leaders do that can be observed and measured. It emphasizes the significance of actions and conduct in influencing the effectiveness of leaders.

Interpersonal Dynamics: The core tenet underscores the interpersonal aspect of leadership, emphasizing that the way leaders engage with and relate to others plays a crucial role in determining their effectiveness.

Behavioral Dimensions

Behavioral Theories identify specific dimensions, behaviors, and styles that contribute to effective leadership. These dimensions provide a framework for understanding the observable actions that leaders engage in.

Three key dimensions are often highlighted:

1. ***Task-Oriented Behaviors:***

    Task-oriented behaviors revolve around the leader's focus on achieving specific goals, tasks, and objectives. This involves planning, organizing, and overseeing the implementation of strategies to accomplish set tasks efficiently.

    A task-oriented leader might set clear performance expectations, establish deadlines, and monitor progress closely to ensure goals are met.

2. ***Relationship-Oriented Behaviors:***

    Relationship-oriented behaviors prioritize building and maintaining positive relationships within the team. Leaders exhibiting these behaviors focus on the well-being, satisfaction, and interpersonal dynamics of team members.

A relationship-oriented leader might emphasize open communication, team building activities, and support mechanisms to create a positive work environment.

3. ***Participative Decision Making:***

Participative decision-making involves involving team members in the decision-making process. Leaders who adopt this behavioral approach seek input, feedback, and collaboration from their team when making decisions.

A leader practicing participative decision-making may conduct team meetings to discuss and gather input on important decisions, fostering a sense of shared ownership.

Importance of Adaptability

Behavioral Theories emphasize the significance of leaders adapting their behaviors to suit different situations and contexts. The importance of adaptability lies in the recognition that a one-size-fits-all approach to leadership may not be effective. Leaders who can flexibly switch between various behaviors are considered more effective, especially in dynamic and ever-changing environments.

Key Points

Situational Responsiveness: Effective leaders understand that different situations require different leadership behaviors. Being adaptable allows leaders to respond appropriately to the unique challenges and demands they face.

Flexibility in Leadership Styles: Behavioral adaptability involves the flexibility to adopt task-oriented, relationship-oriented, or participative behaviors based on the specific needs of the team, project, or organizational context.

Enhanced Leadership Effectiveness: Leaders who can adjust their behaviors demonstrate a higher level of effectiveness, as they can tailor their approach to motivate and engage their team members effectively.

In summary, Behavioral Theories highlight the importance of what leaders do, emphasizing observable behaviors and actions as key determinants of leadership effectiveness. The ability to adapt these behaviors to various situations is considered a critical aspect of effective leadership in dynamic environments.

Exploring the Fundamental Principles of Behavioral Theories in Contemporary Organizational Contexts

Behavioral Theories of leadership offer invaluable insights into the observable actions and behaviors that define effective leadership. These theories are grounded in several fundamental principles that continue to shape leadership practices in contemporary organizational contexts:

- **Focus on Actions and Behaviors**: Behavioral Theories shift the focus from innate traits to observable actions and behaviors. Rather than emphasizing inherent qualities, these theories highlight the importance of what leaders do and how they behave in various situations. In today's fast-paced and dynamic organizational environments, the emphasis on behaviors provides a practical framework for assessing and developing leadership effectiveness.

- **Emphasis on Leadership Styles**: Behavioral Theories recognize that leadership is not a one-size-fits-all concept but can be expressed through a variety of styles. From authoritarian and transactional to democratic and transformational, leaders exhibit different behavioral patterns that influence their effectiveness. Understanding and adapting leadership styles to suit the needs of the organization and its stakeholders is crucial in contemporary organizational contexts characterized by diversity and complexity.

- **Contingency and Situational Factors**: Behavioral Theories acknowledge the role of situational factors in shaping leadership behaviors and outcomes. Leaders must adapt their behaviors based on the demands of the situation, the characteristics of their team members, and the organizational context. In today's ever-changing landscape, where organizations face diverse challenges and opportunities, leaders must exhibit flexibility and agility in their approach to leadership.

- **Importance of Communication and Relationship-building**: Effective communication and relationship-building are central tenets of Behavioral Theories. Leaders who excel in these areas foster trust, collaboration, and engagement within their teams and across the organization. In contemporary organizational contexts characterized by interconnectedness and collaboration, leaders must prioritize open, transparent communication and cultivate strong interpersonal relationships to drive success.

- **Focus on Employee Motivation and Engagement**: Behavioral Theories emphasize the role of leaders in motivating and engaging their employees. By understanding the individual needs, preferences, and aspirations of their team members, leaders can tailor their behaviors to inspire and empower them to perform at their best. In today's knowledge-based economy, where talent retention and engagement are critical to organizational success, effective leadership behaviors play a central role in driving employee satisfaction and productivity.

- **Continuous Learning and Adaptation**: Behavioral Theories underscore the importance of continuous learning and adaptation in leadership development. Leaders must be willing to reflect on their behaviors, seek feedback, and engage in ongoing learning and development activities to enhance their effectiveness. In contemporary organizational contexts characterized by rapid change and disruption, leaders who embrace a growth mindset and demonstrate a commitment to self-improvement are better equipped to navigate challenges and seize opportunities.

In summary, the fundamental principles of Behavioral Theories provide a practical framework for understanding and developing effective leadership behaviors in contemporary organizational contexts. By focusing on observable actions, adapting to situational factors, prioritizing communication and relationship-building, motivating and engaging employees, and embracing continuous learning and adaptation, leaders can enhance their effectiveness and drive success in today's dynamic and complex business environment.

Real Life Examples Illustrating Leaders who Exemplify Behavioral Theories of Leadership

Below few examples provide tangible illustrations of how leaders apply specific behaviors in alignment with Behavioral Theories. Readers can use these cases to understand how different behavioral approaches impact leadership effectiveness in diverse contexts.

1. **Elon Musk's Task-Oriented Leadership at SpaceX:**

Behavioral Focus: Task-Oriented Leadership

Elon Musk, CEO of SpaceX, is known for his task-oriented leadership style, particularly in the context of ambitious space exploration goals. Musk emphasizes meticulous planning, execution of complex tasks, and a results-driven approach to achieve SpaceX's objectives.

Observable Behaviors:

- Strategic Planning: Musk is involved in detailed planning for SpaceX's missions, ensuring that every aspect is meticulously organized.
- Efficiency Emphasis: The focus on cost-effectiveness and operational efficiency is evident in SpaceX's achievements, aligning with task-oriented behaviors.

Impact:

- Successful Rocket Launches: SpaceX's consistent success in launching and landing rockets reflects Musk's emphasis on task efficiency and goal achievement.
- Innovation and Advancements: Musk's task-oriented approach has driven innovation, resulting in reusable rocket technology and lowering the cost of space exploration.

2. **Sheryl Sandberg's Relationship-Oriented Leadership at Facebook:**

Behavioral Focus: Relationship-Oriented Leadership

Sheryl Sandberg, ex COO of Facebook, exemplified relationship-oriented leadership by prioritizing team dynamics, collaboration, and employee well-being. Sandberg emphasized building strong interpersonal relationships to foster a positive and inclusive work environment.

Observable Behaviors:

- Employee Support: Sandberg was known for her advocacy of employee well-being, including initiatives like paid parental leave and support for work-life balance.
- Team Collaboration: She encouraged collaboration and open communication within teams, emphasizing the importance of positive relationships.

Impact:

- Positive Work Culture: Facebook's work culture reflects a strong emphasis on relationships and collaboration, contributing to employee satisfaction.
- Team Engagement: Sandberg's leadership approach has been associated with high levels of employee engagement and a sense of belonging.

3. **Jeff Bezos's Participative Leadership at Amazon:**

Behavioral Focus: Participative Leadership

Jeff Bezos, founder, and former CEO of Amazon, demonstrates participative leadership by actively involving employees in decision-making processes. Bezos encourages open communication and values input from team members across the organization.

Observable Behaviors:

- Open Door Policy: Bezos maintains an open-door policy, welcoming input and feedback from employees at all levels.
- Data-Driven Decision-Making: Amazon's emphasis on data-driven decision-making involves employees

in analyzing and interpreting data to inform strategic choices.

Impact:

- Innovation and Adaptability: Amazon's culture of participative decision-making fosters innovation and adaptability, enabling the company to respond effectively to market changes.
- Employee Empowerment: Bezos's participative leadership style contributes to a sense of empowerment among Amazon employees, promoting a collaborative and innovative work environment.

What motivates individuals to adopt a Behavioral theory approach to leadership

Several factors can motivate individuals to adopt a Behavioral Theory approach to leadership:

1. **Focus on Action and Results:**

   Behavioral Theory emphasizes observable actions and behaviors rather than innate traits or characteristics. Individuals motivated by results and outcomes may be drawn to this approach as it provides a practical framework for understanding and achieving leadership effectiveness through tangible behaviors and actions.

2. **Desire for Flexibility and Adaptability:**

   Behavioral Theory recognizes the importance of adapting leadership behaviors to suit different situations and contexts. Leaders who value flexibility and adaptability may be attracted to this approach as it allows them to adjust their behaviors based on the demands of the situation, the needs of their team members, and the organizational context.

3. **Empowerment and Collaboration**: Behavioral Theory emphasizes the importance of communication, relationship-building, and employee engagement in leadership effectiveness. Leaders who prioritize empowerment, collaboration, and inclusivity may be drawn to this approach as it provides strategies for fostering trust, collaboration, and engagement within their teams and across the organization.

4. **Focus on Continuous Improvement**: Behavioral Theory encourages leaders to reflect on their behaviors, seek feedback, and engage in ongoing learning and development activities to enhance their effectiveness. Individuals who value continuous improvement and personal growth may be motivated to adopt this approach as it provides opportunities for self-reflection, learning, and skill development.

5. **Recognition of Situational Factors**: Behavioral Theory acknowledges the influence of situational factors on leadership behaviors and outcomes. Leaders who recognize the importance of context and adaptability in leadership may be inclined to adopt this approach as it provides a framework for understanding and navigating diverse challenges and opportunities within the organization.

6. **Alignment with Organizational Values**: Behavioral Theory emphasizes communication, collaboration, and employee engagement, which are often aligned with organizational values such as transparency, teamwork, and innovation. Leaders who are committed to upholding and promoting these values within the organization may be motivated to

adopt a Behavioral Theory approach to leadership as it aligns with their personal and organizational values.

Overall, individuals may be motivated to adopt a Behavioral Theory approach to leadership due to its focus on action and results, flexibility and adaptability, empowerment and collaboration, continuous improvement, recognition of situational factors, and alignment with organizational values. By embracing this approach, leaders can enhance their effectiveness and drive success in today's dynamic and complex organizational environments.

Manifestation of Behavioral Theory Leadership framework in day-to-day Leadership practices

The manifestation of Behavioral Theory in day-to-day leadership practices is evident across various dimensions of leadership behavior and interactions. Here's how the principles of Behavioral Theory translate into practical leadership actions:

1. **Communication and Relationship-building**: Behavioral Theory emphasizes the importance of effective communication and relationship-building in leadership. Leaders who adhere to this framework prioritize open, transparent communication with their team members and stakeholders. They actively listen to their concerns, provide constructive feedback, and foster an environment where ideas and opinions are valued. By building strong relationships based on trust and mutual respect, these leaders create a supportive and collaborative work culture.

2. **Adaptive Leadership Styles**: Behavioral Theory recognizes that effective leaders adapt their leadership styles to suit different situations and contexts. Leaders who embody this principle are flexible in their approach, employing a range

of leadership styles—from directive and authoritative to democratic and participative—based on the needs of their team and the demands of the situation. They recognize that there is no one-size-fits-all approach to leadership and adjust their behaviors accordingly to achieve the best outcomes.

3. **Employee Motivation and Engagement**: Behavioral Theory underscores the importance of motivating and engaging employees to drive performance and productivity. Leaders who subscribe to this framework actively involve their team members in decision-making processes, delegate responsibilities, and provide opportunities for growth and development. They recognize and reward individual and team achievements, fostering a sense of ownership and commitment among their employees.

4. **Conflict Resolution and Problem-solving**: Behavioral Theory provides strategies for effectively managing conflicts and solving problems within the team. Leaders who embrace this framework approach conflicts constructively, seeking win-win solutions that address the underlying issues and preserve relationships. They encourage open dialogue, facilitate brainstorming sessions, and leverage the diverse perspectives of team members to identify creative solutions to complex challenges.

5. **Role Modeling and Mentorship**: Behavioral Theory emphasizes the importance of leaders serving as role models and mentors for their team members. Leaders who embody this principle lead by example, demonstrating the behaviors and values they expect from others. They invest time and effort in mentoring and coaching their team members, providing guidance, support, and opportunities for skill

development. Through their actions and behaviors, they inspire and empower others to reach their full potential.

6. **Continuous Learning and Development**: Behavioral Theory encourages leaders to engage in continuous learning and development to enhance their effectiveness. Leaders who adhere to this framework actively seek feedback from their team members, peers, and supervisors, and use it as a catalyst for growth and improvement. They invest in their own professional development, attending training programs, workshops, and seminars to acquire new skills and knowledge that will benefit themselves and their team.

In summary, the principles of Behavioral Theory manifest in day-to-day leadership practices through effective communication and relationship-building, adaptive leadership styles, employee motivation and engagement, conflict resolution and problem-solving, role modeling and mentorship, and continuous learning and development. Leaders who embrace these principles create positive work environments, inspire their team members, and drive organizational success.

Strategies for cultivating Behavioral Theory framework in leadership

Cultivating the Behavioral Theory framework in leadership involves focusing on observable behaviors and actions that contribute to effective leadership. Here are strategies for cultivating the Behavioral Theory framework in leadership:

1. **Leadership Development Programs:**

   - Implement leadership development programs that emphasize the importance of specific behaviors associated with effective leadership, such as active listening, clear communication, empathy, and conflict resolution.

- Offer workshops, seminars, and training sessions focused on developing behavioral competencies essential for effective leadership, such as assertiveness, adaptability, delegation, and decision-making.

2. **Role Modeling and Mentorship:**

- Encourage leaders to serve as positive role models by demonstrating desired behaviors and leading by example. Provide opportunities for aspiring leaders to observe and learn from experienced leaders who exhibit effective leadership behaviors.

- Facilitate mentorship relationships between seasoned leaders and emerging leaders, where mentors can provide guidance, feedback, and support to help mentees develop their behavioral competencies and leadership skills.

3. **Feedback and Coaching:**

- Establish a culture of regular feedback and coaching, where leaders receive constructive feedback on their behaviors and are provided with opportunities for professional growth and development.

- Train managers and supervisors to deliver feedback effectively, focusing on specific behaviors and providing actionable recommendations for improvement. Offer coaching and support to help leaders address areas for development and enhance their leadership effectiveness.

4. **Team Building and Collaboration:**

- Foster a collaborative and inclusive work environment where leaders encourage teamwork, collaboration, and mutual respect among team members. Promote open communication, shared decision-making, and a sense of belonging within teams.

- Provide opportunities for leaders to engage in team-building activities, workshops, and group exercises aimed at strengthening interpersonal relationships, building trust, and enhancing collaboration among team members.

5. **Conflict Resolution and Problem-Solving**:

- Equip leaders with the skills and techniques needed to effectively resolve conflicts and address challenges within their teams and organizations. Provide training in conflict resolution strategies, negotiation techniques, and problem-solving methodologies.

- Encourage leaders to adopt a proactive approach to identifying and addressing conflicts early, fostering open dialogue, and facilitating constructive resolutions that promote harmony and cooperation among team members.

6. **Performance Management and Recognition**:

- Establish clear performance expectations and standards aligned with desired behavioral outcomes for leadership effectiveness. Regularly assess leaders' performance against these criteria and provide feedback on their progress and areas for improvement.

- Recognize and reward leaders who demonstrate desired behaviors and contribute to a positive work environment. Celebrate examples of leadership excellence and highlight individuals who exemplify the organization's values and behavioral expectations.

7. **Continuous Learning and Improvement:**

- Encourage leaders to engage in continuous learning and self-improvement efforts to enhance their behavioral competencies and leadership effectiveness. Provide access to resources such as books, articles, podcasts, and online courses on leadership and behavioral psychology.

- Foster a growth mindset among leaders, encouraging them to embrace challenges, seek feedback, and learn from both successes and failures. Create a culture that values learning, innovation, and personal development as essential components of effective leadership.

By implementing these strategies, organizations can effectively cultivate the Behavioral Theory framework in leadership, enabling leaders to develop and demonstrate the behaviors and actions necessary to inspire, motivate, and lead others effectively.

Behavioral Theory – My Observation and Experience

In the realm of corporate leadership, theories often find their true resonance when translated into real-life experiences. Allow me to share a story that encapsulates the essence of Behavioral Theory, drawing from my own journey in a corporate leadership role.

Around seven years ago, I found myself leading a cross-functional team tasked with launching a critical project that would significantly impact our organization's top line as well as tax compliance status. The project was complex, with multiple stakeholders, tight deadlines, and competing priorities—a situation ripe for challenges and conflicts.

As I navigated the intricacies of leading this diverse team, I found myself leaning heavily on the principles of Behavioral Theory. One aspect that stood out was the emphasis on effective communication and relationship-building.

Recognizing the importance of fostering open dialogue and collaboration, I made a conscious effort to create a culture of transparency and trust within the team. I encouraged team members to voice their opinions, share their concerns, and contribute their ideas freely. Through regular team meetings, one-on-one discussions, and informal gatherings, I sought to build strong relationships based on mutual respect and understanding.

The impact of this approach became evident as the project progressed. Despite the inevitable challenges and setbacks, the team remained cohesive and committed, rallying together to overcome obstacles and achieve our shared goals. The foundation of trust and collaboration we had built enabled us to navigate through uncertainties and complexities with resilience and determination.

Another aspect of Behavioral Theory that resonated deeply with me was the recognition of situational factors and the need for adaptive leadership styles. As the project unfolded, I found myself adjusting my leadership approach based on the evolving needs of the team and the demands of the situation.

During times of uncertainty or ambiguity, I adopted a more participative leadership style, soliciting input from team members and involving them in decision-making processes. Conversely, when quick decisions were required, I shifted to a more directive approach, providing clear guidance and direction to keep the team focused and aligned.

This ability to adapt my leadership style to suit the circumstances proved invaluable in keeping the project on track and maintaining team morale during challenging times.

Reflecting on this experience, I realized how the principles of Behavioral Theory had guided and shaped my leadership approach in tangible ways. By prioritizing effective communication, relationship-building, and adaptive leadership styles, I was able to lead my team successfully through a complex and demanding project, achieving our objectives while strengthening bonds and fostering a culture of collaboration.

As I continue on my leadership journey, I carry with me the invaluable lessons learned from this experience—lessons that underscore the timeless relevance and practical applicability of Behavioral Theory in real-world leadership contexts. Through observation, reflection, and practice, we can harness the power of Behavioral Theory to inspire, motivate, and empower those we lead, driving organizational success and creating lasting impact in the corporate world.

Conclusion

As we draw the curtains on our exploration of Behavioral Theory in leadership, I find myself reflecting on the profound insights and transformative experiences that have shaped our understanding of effective leadership behaviors. This chapter has been a journey of discovery—a journey that has illuminated the path to leadership excellence through the lens of observable actions and behaviors.

Through the anecdotes, principles, and personal reflections shared in these pages, we have uncovered the essence of Behavioral Theory and its profound impact on day-to-day leadership practices. From the importance of effective communication and relationship-building to the adaptive nature of leadership styles, Behavioral Theory has provided us with a practical framework for navigating the complexities of leadership in contemporary organizational contexts.

My own experiences have served as a testament to the enduring relevance and practical applicability of Behavioral Theory in real-world leadership situations. Whether leading a cross-functional team through a critical project or navigating through challenging times with resilience and adaptability, I have witnessed firsthand the power of effective leadership behaviors in driving organizational success and fostering a culture of collaboration and innovation.

As we bid farewell to this chapter, let us carry with us the lessons learned and the insights gained, weaving them into the fabric of our own leadership journeys. May we continue to embrace the principles of Behavioral Theory—prioritizing effective communication, fostering strong relationships, adapting our leadership styles to suit the situation, and nurturing a culture of continuous learning and improvement.

In the ever-evolving landscape of leadership theory, Behavioral Theory stands as a beacon of guidance and inspiration—a reminder that effective leadership is not merely about innate traits or charisma but about the tangible actions and behaviors that inspire, motivate, and empower others to achieve greatness.

As we embark on the next chapter of our leadership journey, let us do so with renewed clarity, purpose, and conviction, knowing that by embodying the principles of Behavioral Theory, we can lead with authenticity, integrity, and impact, leaving a lasting legacy of leadership excellence in our world.

Practical Exercises and Reflection Questions

These exercises and reflection questions are designed to encourage readers to actively apply and critically reflect on the concepts discussed in this chapter. They aim to bridge the gap between theory and practical application, fostering a deeper understanding of how leadership frameworks can be valuable tools in real-world leadership scenarios.

1. **Behavioral Self-Assessment:**

   - **Exercise:** Reflect on your own leadership behaviors and identify whether you lean more towards task-oriented, relationship-oriented, or participative behaviors.
   - **Reflection Questions:**
     - ✓ In what situations do you naturally exhibit task-oriented behaviors?
     - ✓ How do you approach building relationships within your team or organization?
     - ✓ Have you actively sought input from team members in decision-making processes?

2. **Behavioral Impact Analysis:**

   - **Exercise:** Analyze a recent leadership decision or action and assess its impact on team dynamics and outcomes.
   - **Reflection Questions:**
     - ✓ How did your behavior align with either task-oriented, relationship-oriented, or participative approaches?
     - ✓ What was the impact of your behavior on team motivation and productivity?
     - ✓ Are there alternative behaviors that might have yielded different results?

3. **Behavioral Adaptability Challenge:**

   - **Exercise:** Identify a current leadership challenge or project and deliberately choose a behavioral approach that may be different from your default style.
   - **Reflection Questions:**

     - ✓ How did intentionally adopting a different behavioral approach impact the team's response?
     - ✓ Were there any unexpected benefits or challenges associated with the change in behavior?
     - ✓ How can you adapt your leadership behaviors to suit the specific demands of different situations?

4. **Team Feedback Gathering:**

   - **Exercise:** Solicit feedback from team members regarding your leadership behaviors, asking them to identify patterns they observe.
   - **Reflection Questions:**

     - ✓ What commonalities or differences emerge in the feedback regarding your leadership behaviors?
     - ✓ Are there specific behaviors that team members appreciate or find challenging?
     - ✓ How can you leverage positive behaviors and address any areas of improvement?

5. **Behavioral Style Exploration:**

   - **Exercise:** Choose a leader you admire and analyze their observable behaviors to identify whether they exhibit task-oriented, relationship-oriented, or participative tendencies.

- **Reflection Questions:**

  ✓ What specific behaviors of the admired leader align with the three behavioral approaches?
  ✓ How might adopting some of these behaviors enhance your own leadership effectiveness?
  ✓ Are there aspects of their behavior that challenge conventional notions of leadership?

6. **Behavioral Flexibility Action Plan:**

- **Exercise:** Develop a plan to enhance your behavioral flexibility by intentionally practicing different approaches in various leadership situations.

- **Reflection Questions:**

  ✓ How can you incorporate elements of task-oriented, relationship-oriented, and participative behaviors into your leadership toolkit?
  ✓ What specific actions can you take to adapt your behaviors based on the unique demands of your team and organization?
  ✓ How will you measure the success of your efforts in enhancing behavioral flexibility?

Chapter 5

Contingency Theories

In the dynamic landscape of leadership theory, Contingency Theories stand as pillars of understanding, recognizing the importance of adapting leadership approaches to fit the specific demands of different situations. In this chapter, we embark on a journey to explore the nuanced complexities of Contingency Theories, delving into the fundamental principles that govern leadership flexibility and its impact on organizational effectiveness.

Contingency Theories of leadership offer a perspective that acknowledges the diverse and ever-changing nature of organizational environments. Unlike traditional theories that prescribe a one-size-fits-all approach to leadership, Contingency Theories propose that effective leadership is contingent upon the unique characteristics of the situation at hand.

In this chapter, we delve into the core concepts of Contingency Theories, exploring how factors such as the nature of the task, the characteristics of the followers, and the situational context influence leadership effectiveness. Through real-life examples, case studies, and practical insights, we aim to unravel the complexities of adaptive leadership and provide guidance for leaders seeking to navigate the complexities of today's dynamic organizational landscapes.

Join us as we unravel the intricacies of Contingency Theories, uncovering the keys to leadership flexibility and effectiveness in an ever-changing world.

Defining Contingency Theories

Contingency Theories represent a paradigm shift in the understanding of leadership, challenging the conventional wisdom that a singular leadership style can be universally effective. At the core of Contingency Theories is the acknowledgment that leadership is contingent upon a variety of factors, and its effectiveness is context specific. This section explores in-depth the defining characteristics of Contingency Theories, emphasizing the rejection of a one-size-fits-all approach and the recognition of the dynamic nature of leadership.

Rejecting Universality

Unlike earlier leadership theories that sought to identify a universal set of traits or behaviors associated with effective leadership, Contingency Theories assert that there is no one-size-fits-all formula for leadership success. The effectiveness of a particular leadership style is not universal but contingent upon the specific circumstances and variables at play.

Situational Dependency

Contingency Theories posit that the success of a leadership style depends on the situation at hand. Different situations require different leadership approaches. What may be effective in a stable, routine task may not be suitable for a rapidly changing or crisis situation. This acknowledgment of situational dependency introduces a layer of complexity to the understanding of leadership.

Multitude of Variables

Leadership effectiveness, according to Contingency Theories, is influenced by a multitude of variables. These variables may include the nature of the task, the characteristics of the followers, the organizational culture, the level of task structure, and the leader's position power, among others. The interplay of these variables determines the most appropriate leadership style for a given situation.

Adaptability and Responsiveness

At the heart of Contingency Theories is the concept of adaptability. Successful leaders must be adaptable and responsive to the unique demands presented by each circumstance. This adaptability involves a willingness to assess the specific situation, diagnose the relevant variables, and adjust one's leadership style accordingly. It requires leaders to move beyond a rigid adherence to a preferred style and to be open to modifying their approach based on the needs of the moment.

Complexity of Leadership

Contingency Theories highlight the inherent complexity of leadership. Leaders are tasked with navigating a dynamic and ever-changing landscape, and their effectiveness hinges on their ability to comprehend and respond to this complexity. This complexity is not seen as a hindrance but as an inherent aspect of leadership that requires a sophisticated and nuanced approach.

Unique Demands of Each Circumstance

The defining feature of Contingency Theories is the emphasis on the unique demands of each circumstance. Leadership effectiveness is not only about possessing a set of predefined skills or characteristics but about recognizing and addressing the specific challenges and opportunities presented by the context. Leaders must tailor their behaviors and decisions to the intricacies of each situation.

In essence, defining Contingency Theories involves a paradigm shift towards recognizing and embracing the dynamic, context-specific nature of leadership. Leaders who grasp the principles of Contingency Theories are not bound by a fixed set of rules but are empowered to navigate the complexities of leadership with agility, adaptability, and a keen understanding of the unique demands of each circumstance.

Navigating the Landscape of Contingency Models

We will explore key Contingency Models that have shaped the discourse on leadership. Fiedler's Contingency Model, Hersey-Blanchard's Situational Leadership Theory, and the Path-Goal Theory are among the models that shed light on how leaders can strategically adapt their approaches based on situational nuances. These Contingency Theory models provide distinct lenses through which leaders can understand and adapt their approaches based on situational factors. By considering the nuances of leader-follower relationships, task structures, and readiness levels, leaders can enhance their effectiveness in diverse contexts. The real-world examples showcase how these models can be applied successfully, offering valuable insights for leaders navigating the complexities of their roles.

1. **Fiedler's Contingency Model:**

   Key Principles:

   Leader-Member Relations: Fiedler's model places a significant emphasis on the quality of the relationship between the leader and group members. The theory asserts that leader effectiveness is contingent on the level of trust, respect, and confidence followers have in their leader.

   Task Structure: Task structure refers to the clarity of the group's goals and the procedures for achieving those goals. Fiedler argued that in situations of high or low task structure, certain leadership styles are more effective.

Leader Position Power: The degree of power vested in the leader by the organization also plays a crucial role. Leaders with strong position power can more easily influence and guide their team.

Leadership Styles:

Task Oriented Leaders: Focused on achieving goals and maintaining task structure. They excel in situations of high or low task structure.

Relationship Oriented Leaders: Emphasize building strong leader-member relations and are effective in situations of moderate task structure.

Real World Application:

Example: Southwest Airlines is often cited as an example aligning with Fiedler's model. The task-oriented leadership approach of its founder, Herb Kelleher, was effective in the dynamic and highly competitive airline industry.

2. **Hersey-Blanchard's Situational Leadership Theory:**

Key Principles:

Readiness of Followers: Hersey and Blanchard proposed that effective leadership is contingent on the readiness or maturity of followers. Readiness is determined by the followers' ability and willingness to perform a specific task.

Leadership Styles: The model identifies four leadership styles based on combinations of high or low task behavior and high or low relationship behavior. The leader adapts their style to match the readiness of followers.

Leadership Styles:

Telling: High task, low relationship – for followers with low readiness.

Selling: High task, high relationship – for followers with moderate readiness.

Participating: Low task, high relationship – for followers with high readiness.

Delegating: Low task, low relationship – for followers with very high readiness.

Real World Application:

Example: Lou Gerstner's leadership at IBM during its transformation is often considered a case where situational leadership was applied effectively. Gerstner adjusted his leadership style based on the readiness of employees for significant organizational change.

3. **Path Goal Theory:**

Key Principles:

Clarifying Paths: Leaders are responsible for clarifying the path to goal achievement by removing obstacles and making the journey clear and understandable for followers.

Removing Obstacles: Effective leaders identify and eliminate barriers that hinder progress. This involves addressing challenges and ensuring that followers can navigate the path with minimal hindrance.

Providing Support: Leaders offer support to enhance followers' motivation and confidence. This support can be emotional, informational, or instrumental, depending on the needs of the followers.

Leadership Styles:

Directive Leadership: Provides clear guidance and expectations.

Supportive Leadership: Demonstrates concern for the well-being of followers.

Participative Leadership: Involves followers in decision-making.

Achievement-Oriented Leadership: Sets challenging goals and expects high.

Real World Application:

Example: Steve Jobs at Apple exemplifies aspects of the Path-Goal Theory. Jobs was known for setting ambitious goals (achievement-oriented), providing a clear vision (directive), and fostering a culture of innovation (supportive).

Real Life Examples Illustrating Leaders who Exemplify Contingency Theories of Leadership

Below a few real-life examples showcase how leaders apply Contingency Theories to adapt their leadership styles based on the specific demands of their industries, organizations, and teams. The ability to navigate diverse situations with flexibility and adaptability contributes to their effectiveness as leaders.

1. **Angela Merkel – Former Chancellor of Germany (Fiedler's Contingency Model):**

   Fiedler's Contingency Model emphasizes the importance of leader-member relations, task structure, and leader position power. Angela Merkel, during her tenure as the Chancellor of Germany, demonstrated adaptability in her leadership style based on the changing political landscape.

Merkel's leadership was characterized by a pragmatic and adaptive approach. She navigated complex European political situations with a focus on consensus-building, demonstrating both relationship-oriented and task-oriented behaviors as the situation required.

2. **Bill Gates – Microsoft (Hersey-Blanchard's Situational Leadership Theory):**

Hersey-Blanchard's Situational Leadership Theory is based on the readiness of followers. Bill Gates, co-founder of Microsoft, exemplifies situational leadership by adapting his leadership style based on the evolving needs of the technology industry and the maturity of his teams.

Gates was known for his directive leadership style during the early stages of Microsoft's growth, providing clear guidance and vision. As the company matured, he transitioned to a more participative and empowering leadership style, encouraging innovation and collaboration.

3. **Mary Barra – General Motors (Path-Goal Theory):**

The Path-Goal Theory emphasizes the leader's role in clarifying paths, removing obstacles, and providing support. Mary Barra, CEO of General Motors, exemplifies path-goal leadership by navigating the automotive industry with a focus on goal clarity, obstacle removal, and support for her team.

Barra led General Motors through significant challenges, clarifying the company's goals for innovation and sustainability. She addressed obstacles by initiating cultural changes and providing support for initiatives such as electric vehicle development, aligning leadership behavior with the company's strategic direction.

What motivates individuals to adopt a Contingency theory approach to leadership

Several factors can motivate individuals to adopt a Contingency Theory approach to leadership:

1. **Recognition of Situational Complexity**: Individuals may be motivated to adopt a Contingency Theory approach when they recognize the complexity of organizational environments. Contingency Theory acknowledges that no single leadership style or approach is universally effective and emphasizes the need for leaders to adapt their behaviors to fit the specific demands of different situations. Leaders who appreciate the intricacies of organizational contexts may be drawn to this approach as it provides a framework for navigating diverse challenges and opportunities effectively.

2. **Desire for Effective Leadership Practices**: Individuals who aspire to be effective leaders are often motivated to adopt a Contingency Theory approach. This framework offers insights into the factors that influence leadership effectiveness, such as the nature of the task, the characteristics of the followers, and the situational context. By understanding these factors and adapting their leadership behaviors accordingly, individuals can enhance their effectiveness as leaders and drive better outcomes for their teams and organizations.

3. **Flexibility and Adaptability**: Contingency Theory emphasizes the importance of flexibility and adaptability in

leadership. Leaders who value these traits may be drawn to this approach as it encourages them to adjust their behaviors and strategies based on the demands of the situation. By being flexible and adaptable, leaders can respond effectively to changing circumstances, seize opportunities, and overcome challenges, ultimately leading to improved organizational performance.

4. **Desire for Personal and Organizational Growth**: Individuals who are committed to personal and organizational growth may be motivated to adopt a Contingency Theory approach. This framework encourages leaders to continually assess and adapt their behaviors in response to changing circumstances, fostering a culture of learning and improvement within the organization. By embracing this approach, leaders can contribute to the growth and success of their teams and organizations over time.

5. **Alignment with Organizational Values**: Contingency Theory aligns with certain organizational values, such as innovation, agility, and responsiveness. Leaders who are committed to upholding these values may be motivated to adopt this approach as it enables them to lead in a manner that is consistent with the organization's ethos. By aligning their leadership practices with organizational values, leaders can foster a sense of unity, purpose, and alignment within the organization.

Overall, individuals may be motivated to adopt a Contingency Theory approach to leadership due to its recognition of situational complexity, emphasis on effective leadership practices, promotion of flexibility and adaptability, support for personal and organizational growth, and alignment with organizational values. By embracing this approach, leaders can enhance their effectiveness, drive better outcomes, and contribute to the overall success of their teams and organizations.

Manifestation of Contingency Theory Leadership framework in day-to-day Leadership practices

The manifestation of Contingency Theory in day-to-day leadership practices is evident in several key areas:

- **Adaptive Leadership Styles**: Leaders who embrace Contingency Theory understand that different situations require different leadership approaches. They are adept at assessing the specific demands of each situation and adapting their leadership style accordingly. For example, in a crisis situation, they may adopt a more directive approach to provide clear guidance and direction, whereas in a creative brainstorming session, they may adopt a more participative style to encourage collaboration and idea generation.

- **Situational Analysis**: Contingency Theory emphasizes the importance of situational analysis in leadership decision-making. Leaders who adhere to this framework are skilled at assessing the unique characteristics of each situation, including the nature of the task, the capabilities of their team members, and the external environment. They use this analysis to inform their leadership approach, making decisions that are tailored to the specific context.

- **Flexibility and Adaptability**: One of the key principles of Contingency Theory is flexibility and adaptability. Leaders who embody this framework are agile in their approach, able to quickly adjust their behaviors and strategies in response to changing circumstances. They are open to new ideas and perspectives, willing to experiment with different approaches, and able to pivot when necessary to achieve the desired outcomes.

- **Customized Leadership Practices**: Contingency Theory encourages leaders to customize their leadership practices to fit the needs of their team and organization. Leaders who follow this framework take a personalized approach to leadership, recognizing that what works in one situation may not work in another. They are attentive to the unique strengths, weaknesses, and preferences of their team members and tailor their leadership practices accordingly to maximize effectiveness.

- **Risk Management**: Contingency Theory also involves risk management in leadership decision-making. Leaders who adopt this framework carefully assess the potential risks and rewards associated with different courses of action and make decisions that minimize risk while maximizing the likelihood of success. They are proactive in identifying and addressing potential obstacles and challenges, ensuring that their team is well-prepared to handle whatever comes their way.

- **Continuous Learning and Improvement**: Leaders who embrace Contingency Theory are committed to continuous learning and improvement. They regularly reflect on their leadership practices, seeking feedback from their team members and peers, and using this feedback to refine their approach over time. They are humble enough to acknowledge that there is always room for growth and strive to continuously enhance their leadership skills and capabilities.

Overall, the manifestation of Contingency Theory in day-to-day leadership practices involves adaptive leadership styles, situational analysis, flexibility and adaptability, customized leadership practices, risk management, and continuous learning and improvement. Leaders who embody this framework are able to navigate the complexities of organizational environments effectively, driving success and achieving positive outcomes for their teams and organizations.

Strategies for cultivating Contingency Theory framework in leadership

Cultivating the Contingency Theory framework in leadership involves recognizing the importance of adapting leadership styles and approaches based on the specific context and circumstances. Here are strategies for cultivating the Contingency Theory framework in leadership:

1. **Situation Analysis and Assessment:**

    - Train leaders to assess and analyze various situational factors, including the organization's culture, goals, structure, and external environment, to determine the most appropriate leadership approach.
    - Encourage leaders to conduct thorough assessments of their teams, considering factors such as team dynamics, member competencies, task complexity, and project requirements, to tailor their leadership style accordingly.

2. **Flexible Leadership Styles:**

    - Educate leaders about different leadership styles and approaches, such as directive, supportive, participative, and delegative, and help them understand when each style is most effective based on the situation.

- Encourage leaders to be flexible and adaptable in their leadership approach, recognizing that there is no one-size-fits-all solution and that leadership styles should be adjusted based on the needs and characteristics of the situation.

3. **Contingency Planning and Decision-Making**:

   - Train leaders to develop contingency plans and strategies to address potential challenges, risks, and uncertainties that may arise in different situations. Encourage leaders to anticipate various scenarios and prepare appropriate responses.

   - Foster a culture of proactive decision-making, where leaders are empowered to make timely and informed decisions based on the specific circumstances and objectives of the situation.

4. **Communication and Stakeholder Engagement**:

   - Emphasize the importance of effective communication and stakeholder engagement in contingency leadership. Train leaders to communicate clearly, openly, and transparently with team members, stakeholders, and other key parties, keeping them informed and engaged throughout the decision-making process.

   - Encourage leaders to seek input and feedback from relevant stakeholders, leveraging their diverse perspectives and expertise to inform decision-making and problem-solving efforts.

5. **Team Development and Empowerment**:

   - Foster the development of self-managing and empowered teams capable of adapting to changing circumstances and taking appropriate actions autonomously.

- Provide leadership development opportunities for team members, empowering them to take on leadership roles and responsibilities as needed and enhancing their capacity to contribute effectively to the team's success.

6. **Continuous Learning and Improvement:**

   - Encourage leaders to engage in continuous learning and professional development to enhance their knowledge, skills, and abilities in navigating complex and dynamic leadership situations.
   - Provide access to training programs, workshops, and resources focused on contingency leadership principles, situational awareness, decision-making strategies, and adaptive leadership practices.

7. **Performance Evaluation and Feedback:**

   - Establish performance metrics and evaluation criteria that reflect the ability of leaders to effectively adapt their leadership style to different situations and contexts.
   - Provide leaders with regular feedback on their performance, highlighting instances where they demonstrated effective contingency leadership behaviors and areas for improvement.

By implementing these strategies, organizations can effectively cultivate the Contingency Theory framework in leadership, enabling leaders to navigate complexity, uncertainty, and change with agility and effectiveness.

Contingency Theory – My Observation and Experience

In the dynamic world of finance, where market conditions can change in an instant, the ability to adapt and respond swiftly is essential for effective leadership. Allow me to share a story from my own experience, highlighting the principles of Contingency Theory in a finance context.

Earlier in my career as a Finance Manager for a multinational corporation, Rentokil India, I was tasked with leading a team responsible for financial planning and analysis. Our primary goal was to develop annual budgets and forecasts that aligned with the company's strategic objectives and financial targets. However, as we delved into the budgeting process, we encountered a significant challenge—an unexpected downturn in the global economy that threatened to impact our revenue projections and profitability targets.

In response to this unforeseen challenge, I recognized the need for a flexible and adaptive leadership approach. Rather than adhering rigidly to our original budgeting timeline and assumptions, I convened an emergency meeting with my team to assess the situation and devise a plan of action. Drawing upon the principles of Contingency Theory, I emphasized the importance of situational analysis and encouraged open dialogue among team members to gather insights and perspectives.

During the meeting, it became apparent that our existing revenue models and assumptions were no longer valid in the current economic climate. Recognizing the need for a swift response, I empowered my team to think creatively and explore alternative scenarios that could mitigate the impact of the downturn on our financial performance.

Through collaborative brainstorming and analysis, we developed a contingency budgeting plan that incorporated various revenue scenarios based on different market conditions. We identified key cost-saving initiatives and investment opportunities that could be implemented to optimize our financial performance in the face of uncertainty.

As we implemented the contingency budgeting plan, I adopted a supportive leadership style, providing guidance and resources to help my team navigate through the challenges ahead. I encouraged open communication and feedback, ensuring that everyone felt empowered to contribute their ideas and perspectives.

Over time, our adaptive approach to financial planning proved to be instrumental in helping the company weather the storm of economic uncertainty. By embracing the principles of Contingency Theory and adapting our leadership approach to fit the specific demands of the situation, we were able to navigate through challenges effectively and achieve our financial objectives.

As I reflect on this journey, I am reminded of the timeless relevance of Contingency Theory in today's corporate landscape. In a world characterized by complexity and uncertainty, leaders who embrace flexibility and adaptability are better equipped to navigate through challenges, seize opportunities, and drive success for their teams and organizations.

This experience has reinforced my belief in the power of Contingency Theory as a guiding framework for effective leadership. By understanding and applying the principles of Contingency Theory, leaders can navigate the complexities of organizational environments with confidence and resilience, achieving positive outcomes and making a lasting impact in the corporate world.

Conclusion

As we conclude our exploration of Contingency Theory in leadership, I am reminded of the profound impact that flexibility and adaptability can have on leadership effectiveness. Through personal experiences, anecdotes, and insights shared in this chapter, we have delved into the dynamic nature of leadership, highlighting the importance of tailoring our approach to fit the specific demands of different situations.

Contingency Theory serves as a guiding framework for leaders in navigating through the complexities of organizational environments, emphasizing the need for situational analysis, flexibility, and adaptability. By recognizing that there is no one-size-fits-all approach to leadership, and embracing a mindset of continuous learning and adjustment, leaders can effectively navigate through challenges, seize opportunities, and drive success for their teams and organizations.

My own journey in leadership has been shaped by the principles of Contingency Theory, as I have learned to adapt my leadership approach to fit the unique characteristics of each situation. Whether facing unexpected challenges in financial planning or navigating through uncertain market conditions, I have witnessed firsthand the transformative power of flexibility and adaptability in leadership.

As we move forward on our leadership journey, let us carry with us the lessons learned from Contingency Theory—embracing flexibility, adapting to change, and responding thoughtfully to the demands of each situation. By doing so, we can navigate through uncertainty with confidence, inspire our teams to greatness, and achieve success in today's ever-evolving organizational landscape.

Practical Exercises and Reflection Questions

These exercises and reflection questions are designed to encourage readers to actively apply and critically reflect on the concepts discussed in this chapter. They aim to bridge the gap between theory and practical application, fostering a deeper understanding of how leadership frameworks can be valuable tools in real-world leadership scenarios.

1. **Reflecting on Leader-Member relations:**

   - **Exercise:** Identify a recent leadership scenario in your experience where the quality of leader-member relations played a significant role. Analyze the impact of these relations on the outcome.

   - **Reflection Questions:**

     ✓ How did the quality of leader-member relations influence the dynamics of the situation?

     ✓ In what ways could you enhance leader-member relations in similar future scenarios?

2. **Analyzing Task Structure:**

   - **Exercise:** Think about a project or task you've led recently. Assess the level of task structure involved – was it highly defined, moderately defined, or unclear?

   - **Reflection Questions:**

     ✓ How did the level of task structure impact your leadership approach?

     ✓ What adjustments could you make in a situation with a different level of task structure?

3. **Considering Leader Position Power:**

- **Exercise.** Reflect on a situation where your positional power as a leader played a significant role. Consider how your authority or lack thereof influenced the outcome.
- **Reflection Questions:**

  ✓ How did your position power impact the response and actions of your team?

  ✓ In what ways can you leverage or augment your position power to enhance leadership effectiveness?

4. **Assessing Follower Readiness (Hersey-Blanchard's Model):**

- **Exercise:** Recall a recent leadership challenge where the readiness level of your team members varied. Assess the readiness of each member in that situation.
- **Reflection Questions:**

  ✓ How did you adapt your leadership style to the varying readiness levels?

  ✓ Are there patterns or trends in your team's readiness levels that you can anticipate in future scenarios?

5. **Clarifying Paths and Removing Obstacles (Path Goal Theory):**

- **Exercise:** Think about a goal you set for your team. Reflect on how you clarified the path and addressed potential obstacles.
- **Reflection Questions:**

  ✓ How did your efforts in clarifying paths contribute to goal achievement?

✓ What obstacles did you encounter, and how did you overcome them to support your team's progress?

6. **Adapting Leadership Styles:**

- **Exercise:** Take an overall inventory of your recent leadership experiences. Identify instances where you consciously adapted your leadership style based on situational factors.

- **Reflection Questions:**

  ✓ What factors influenced your decision to adapt your leadership style?

  ✓ How did the adaptation contribute to positive outcomes or mitigate challenges?

7. **Future Scenario Planning:**

- **Exercise:** Envision a hypothetical future leadership scenario with unique challenges. Apply the principles of Contingency Theories to strategize how you might approach this scenario.

- **Reflection Questions:**

  ✓ What leadership style(s) would be most effective in this hypothetical scenario?

  ✓ How can you proactively prepare for the potential contingencies that may arise?

Chapter 6

Transformational Leadership

Leadership, like an ever-evolving landscape, witnesses the emergence of paradigms that redefine the very essence of guiding and inspiring others. In this intricate tapestry of leadership theories, one concept stands out with unparalleled significance—Transformational Leadership. This chapter embarks on a profound exploration into the realms of Transformational Leadership, a beacon that transcends conventional models, elevating leadership to new heights.

The Magnitude of Transformational Leadership

In the vast expanse of leadership studies, few concepts have captured the collective imagination and scholarly acclaim as intensely as Transformational Leadership. It is not merely a leadership style; it is a transformative force that reshapes how we perceive leadership itself. As we open the doors to this chapter, we are poised to unravel the depths of this transformative paradigm, understanding how leaders harness inspiration and motivation to steer their teams towards extraordinary achievements.

Beyond Tradition, Into Inspiration

Transformational Leadership marks a departure from traditional models. It goes beyond the day-to-day mechanics of management and enters the realm of inspiration and motivation. It is not about simply overseeing tasks; it is about igniting a collective passion that propels teams to exceed their own expectations. This chapter serves as a guide through this transformative journey, shedding light on the defining characteristics and core tenets that distinguish Transformational Leadership from its counterparts.

Inspiration as a Catalyst for Extraordinary Outcomes

At the heart of Transformational Leadership lies the power to inspire. Leaders wielding this paradigm are visionaries who can articulate a compelling narrative that captivates the hearts and minds of their followers. It is about more than just setting goals; it is about creating a shared vision that resonates with the aspirations of each individual within the team. The chapter delves into the artistry of inspiration, exploring how leaders become architects of dreams that drive teams toward exceptional accomplishments.

Motivation Transcending Self-Interest

Transformational Leadership elevates motivation to a level that transcends individual self-interest. It is a call to action that aligns personal aspirations with the collective goals of the organization. Leaders embracing this paradigm cultivate a sense of unity and purpose, fostering a collaborative spirit that propels teams toward a shared destiny. As we journey through this chapter, we will uncover the intricacies of motivation that fuel the transformative engine of leadership.

This chapter is an invitation—an invitation to explore the profound depths of a leadership paradigm that has the potential to reshape destinies. As we navigate through defining characteristics, core tenets, and real-world impact, readers are encouraged to envision the transformative leader within themselves. This exploration is not a mere academic exercise; it is a journey towards unlocking the transformative potential that lies dormant in every leader, waiting to be awakened.

In this chapter, we delve into the core concepts of Transformational Leadership, exploring how visionary leaders inspire and empower their teams to reach new heights of performance and achieve organizational goals. Through real-life examples, case studies, and practical insights, we aim to uncover the secrets of Transformational Leadership and provide guidance for leaders seeking to drive meaningful change within their organizations.

Join us as we unravel the transformative potential of Transformational Leadership, discovering how visionary leaders can inspire, motivate, and empower their teams to create a better future for themselves and their organizations.

Defining Transformational Leadership: A Deep Dive into Visionary Guidance

Definition Unveiled

Transformational Leadership is not a mere managerial technique; it is a profound philosophy of leadership that seeks to transcend the traditional boundaries of management. At its core, it is a style that aspires to instigate positive and profound changes in individuals and organizations. This paradigm places emphasis not on the transactional aspects of leadership but on the transformation of individuals and, by extension, the collective entity. It is a journey that leaders embark upon to inspire their teams to reach beyond self-interest and strive for the greater good.

Characteristics: Illuminating the Essence

1. **Inspirational Motivation:**

   - *Visionary Artistry:* Transformational leaders are architects of vision. They possess the unique ability to articulate a compelling and vivid vision that goes beyond the mundane. This inspirational motivation is not merely about setting goals; it is about painting a picture of a future that resonates with the aspirations and ideals of each team member. The leader becomes a storyteller, weaving a narrative that ignites passion and purpose.

- *Fostering Purpose and Excitement:* The leader's role is to infuse a sense of purpose and excitement within the team. Through words and actions, they cultivate an environment where each member sees themselves as an integral part of a collective journey toward a shared destiny.

2. **Individualized Consideration:**

- *Tailoring Leadership:* Transformational leaders recognize the uniqueness of each team member. Individualized consideration is the practice of tailoring leadership approaches to meet the distinct needs, strengths, and developmental requirements of each follower.

- *Creating a Supportive Ecosystem:* Leaders go beyond the generic, one-size-fits-all approach. They actively engage in understanding the personal and professional aspirations of their team members. This personalized attention creates a supportive ecosystem where individuals feel valued and empowered to contribute their best.

3. **Intellectual Stimulation:**

- *Challenging the Status Quo:* A hallmark of Transformational Leadership is intellectual stimulation. Leaders challenge the status quo, encouraging creativity, critical thinking, and innovation within the team. This goes beyond routine tasks; it involves fostering an environment where new ideas are welcomed, and intellectual growth is nurtured.

- *Promoting Innovation:* Leaders act as catalysts for intellectual advancement. They create spaces for dialogue, debate, and ideation, fostering an atmosphere where team members feel encouraged to contribute their unique perspectives. This commitment to intellectual stimulation propels the team toward continuous improvement and innovation.

4. **Idealized Influence:**

- *Modeling Ethical Standards:* Transformational leaders are not distant figures but individuals who lead by example. Idealized influence is about embodying the ethical standards and values that they wish to instill in their teams.
- *Earning Trust and Respect:* Leaders become role models, earning the trust and respect of their followers through consistent ethical behavior. This influence is not based on coercion but on the genuine admiration that stems from the alignment of the leader's actions with a set of shared values.

In essence, the defining characteristics of Transformational Leadership weave a narrative of visionary guidance, personalized attention, intellectual vigor, and ethical exemplification. As we delve into these characteristics, we unravel the intricacies of a leadership philosophy that transcends transactional interactions and propels individuals and organizations toward transformative growth.

Theoretical Frameworks of Transformation Leadership

Several theoretical frameworks contribute to the understanding of Transformational Leadership. Here are some key theoretical frameworks associated with Transformational Leadership:

1. **Bass's Transformational Leadership Theory:**

   Developed by James MacGregor Burns and later expanded by Bernard M. Bass, this theory is foundational in understanding Transformational Leadership. It identifies four key components of transformational leadership: idealized influence, inspirational motivation, intellectual stimulation, and individualized consideration.

2. **Bass and Riggio's Transformational Leadership Model:**

   Building on the original model, this framework adds transactional leadership elements and further explores the interactions between leaders and followers. It emphasizes the charismatic and inspirational qualities of transformational leaders.

3. **Avolio and Bass's Full Range Leadership Model:**

   This model expands on Bass's work and introduces a continuum of leadership styles ranging from laissez-faire and transactional to transformational leadership. It provides a comprehensive view of leadership behaviors and their impact on organizational outcomes.

4. **Kouzes and Posner's Leadership Challenge Model:**

   Kouzes and Posner's model identifies five practices of exemplary leadership, two of which closely align with transformational leadership principles: "Inspire a Shared Vision" and "Enable Others to Act." Their framework emphasizes the importance of inspiring others and fostering collaboration.

5. **Bass and Steidlmeier's Ethical Leadership Model:**

   This model integrates ethical considerations into the transformational leadership framework. It explores how transformational leaders can influence followers to act ethically and contribute to the well-being of the organization and society.

6. **House's Path-Goal Theory:**

While not exclusively a Transformational Leadership theory, the Path-Goal Theory, developed by Robert House, incorporates transformational leadership elements. It focuses on how leaders can motivate followers by clarifying paths to goals and removing obstacles.

7. **Ling's Global Transformational Leadership Model:**

This model extends the understanding of transformational leadership to a global context. It emphasizes cultural influences and explores how leaders can exhibit transformational behaviors across diverse cultural settings.

8. **Bass and Riggio's Charismatic Leadership Theory:**

Charismatic Leadership is closely related to Transformational Leadership. This theory emphasizes the charismatic qualities of leaders and their ability to inspire and influence followers through their personal charisma.

9. **Yukl's Integrative Leadership Model:**

This model integrates transformational and transactional leadership into a broader framework. It acknowledges the multifaceted nature of leadership and the importance of adapting leadership styles to different situations.

10. **Bennis and Nanus's Visionary Leadership Model:**

Bennis and Nanus propose that visionary leadership, a key aspect of transformational leadership, involves having a clear and compelling vision for the future. This model explores how leaders can articulate and implement a compelling vision to inspire followers.

Real Life Examples Illustrating Leaders who Exemplify Transformational Leadership

Below are a few real-life examples that showcase how leaders from diverse fields have embodied the principles of Transformational Leadership, inspiring and motivating others to achieve extraordinary outcomes:

1. **Martin Luther King Jr.:**

   Visionary Leadership: Martin Luther King Jr. is an iconic example of a transformational leader who inspired positive change on a societal level. His vision for racial equality and justice in the United States during the Civil Rights Movement captivated the hearts and minds of millions.

   Inspirational Motivation: King's speeches, such as the famous "I Have a Dream" speech, were powerful expressions of his visionary ideals. He painted a compelling picture of a future where individuals were judged by their character rather than the color of their skin, inspiring a collective commitment to the values of equality and justice.

   Motivation beyond Self-Interest King's leadership transcended personal interests; he cultivated a sense of collective identity among diverse groups of people, fostering a shared commitment to the larger goal of achieving civil rights for all.

2. **Oprah Winfrey:**

   Individualized Consideration: Oprah Winfrey, a media mogul and philanthropist, exemplifies transformational leadership through her individualized consideration for the needs and aspirations of her audience. Her ability to connect with people on a personal level has contributed to her widespread influence.

Intellectual Stimulation: Winfrey has challenged societal norms through her media platforms, encouraging critical thinking and discussions on various issues. Her book club, for example, has stimulated intellectual growth by promoting literature and fostering a culture of continuous learning.

Idealized Influence: As a public figure, Oprah has served as a role model, earning trust and respect by exemplifying authenticity, resilience, and ethical values. Her influence extends beyond entertainment to inspiring positive personal and societal transformations.

3. **Elon Musk:**

Inspirational Motivation: Elon Musk, the visionary entrepreneur behind companies like SpaceX and Tesla, exemplifies transformational leadership through his ability to articulate and pursue audacious goals. His vision of sustainable energy, interplanetary exploration, and technological innovation has inspired a new era of possibilities.

Intellectual Stimulation: Musk encourages innovation and intellectual exploration within his companies. SpaceX's mission to make life multi-planetary and Tesla's focus on electric vehicles are examples of how Musk challenges the status quo and promotes intellectual growth within his organizations.

Motivation beyond Self-Interest: Musk's leadership extends beyond personal success; he is driven by a larger mission to address pressing global challenges. His commitment to environmental sustainability and space exploration reflects a motivation that transcends individual interests for the collective good.

What motivates individuals to adopt a Transformational approach to leadership

Several factors can motivate individuals to adopt a Transformational approach to leadership:

1. **Desire for Impact and Influence**: Individuals who aspire to make a significant impact and influence positive change within their organizations may be motivated to adopt a Transformational approach to leadership. Transformational leaders have the ability to inspire and motivate others to achieve extraordinary outcomes, empowering them to embrace change and innovation. Leaders who are driven by a desire to leave a legacy and make a difference in the lives of their followers may be drawn to this approach.

2. **Visionary Mindset**: Individuals who possess a visionary mindset and a strong sense of purpose may be naturally inclined towards Transformational leadership. Transformational leaders articulate a compelling vision for the future, inspiring others to rally behind a common cause and work towards shared goals. Leaders who are passionate about creating a better future and driving meaningful change may be motivated to adopt this approach as it aligns with their personal values and aspirations.

3. **Charismatic Personality**: Charisma is often associated with Transformational leadership, as charismatic leaders have a natural ability to inspire and influence others through their

magnetic personality and persuasive communication style. Individuals who possess charisma and charm may be drawn to this leadership approach as it allows them to leverage their innate qualities to inspire and motivate others.

4. **Commitment to Personal Growth**: Transformational leadership emphasizes the importance of personal growth and development, both for leaders and their followers. Leaders who are committed to continuous learning and improvement may be motivated to adopt this approach as it encourages self-reflection, introspection, and growth. Transformational leaders serve as role models for their followers, inspiring them to reach their full potential and achieve excellence.

5. **Alignment with Organizational Values**: Transformational leadership often aligns with certain organizational values, such as innovation, creativity, and excellence. Leaders who are committed to upholding these values and driving organizational success may be motivated to adopt this approach as it fosters a culture of innovation, collaboration, and high performance. By inspiring others to embrace change and pursue excellence, Transformational leaders can contribute to the overall success and growth of their organizations.

Overall, individuals may be motivated to adopt a Transformational approach to leadership due to their desire for impact and influence, visionary mindset, charismatic personality, commitment to personal growth, and alignment with organizational values. By embracing Transformational leadership, leaders can inspire, motivate, and empower others to achieve extraordinary outcomes and create a better future for themselves and their organizations.

Manifestation of Transformational Leadership framework in day-to-day Leadership practices

The manifestation of Transformational Leadership in day-to-day leadership practices is evident across various dimensions of leadership behavior and interactions. Here's how the principles of Transformational Leadership translate into practical actions and behaviors:

1. **Visionary Communication**: Transformational leaders articulate a compelling vision for the future that inspires and motivates their team members. They communicate this vision clearly and passionately, painting a vivid picture of what success looks like and rallying their team around common goals and aspirations. In day-to-day practices, transformational leaders engage in regular communication sessions to reinforce the vision, share progress updates, and celebrate successes, keeping the team aligned and focused on the larger purpose.

2. **Empowerment and Delegation**: Transformational leaders empower their team members by delegating authority and decision-making responsibilities. They trust their team members to take ownership of their work and provide them with the support and resources they need to succeed. In day-to-day practices, transformational leaders actively involve their team members in decision-making processes, encourage them to voice their ideas and opinions, and delegate tasks based on individual strengths and capabilities, fostering a sense of ownership and accountability.

3. **Inspiring and Motivating Others**: Transformational leaders inspire and motivate their team members to perform at their best by setting high standards of excellence and providing

encouragement and support. They lead by example, demonstrating passion, commitment, and resilience in pursuit of the shared vision. In day-to-day practices, transformational leaders recognize and celebrate the achievements of their team members, provide positive feedback and encouragement, and create a supportive and uplifting work environment where individuals feel valued and motivated to contribute their best.

4. **Individualized Consideration**: Transformational leaders show genuine concern and care for the personal and professional development of their team members. They take the time to understand each individual's strengths, weaknesses, and aspirations and provide personalized support and guidance to help them grow and succeed. In day-to-day practices, transformational leaders engage in regular one-on-one meetings with team members to discuss their goals and progress, offer mentorship and coaching, and provide opportunities for learning and development, fostering a culture of continuous growth and improvement.

5. **Intellectual Stimulation**: Transformational leaders encourage creativity and innovation by challenging the status quo and fostering a culture of intellectual stimulation. They encourage their team members to think critically, question assumptions, and explore new ideas and perspectives. In day-to-day practices, transformational leaders facilitate brainstorming sessions, encourage open dialogue and debate, and welcome diverse viewpoints, creating an environment where innovation flourishes and new solutions emerge.

Overall, the manifestation of Transformational Leadership in day-to-day practices involves visionary communication, empowerment and delegation, inspiring and motivating others, individualized consideration, and intellectual stimulation. Leaders who embody this framework create a positive and empowering work environment where individuals are inspired to reach their full potential, teams collaborate effectively, and organizations thrive in a rapidly changing world.

Strategies for cultivating Transformation framework in leadership

Cultivating the Transformational Leadership framework involves fostering leaders' abilities to inspire and motivate others toward achieving common goals, driving positive change, and empowering individuals to reach their full potential. Here are strategies for cultivating the Transformational Leadership framework in leadership:

1. **Visionary Leadership**:

   - Encourage leaders to develop a compelling vision that articulates a clear and inspiring picture of the future. Leaders should communicate this vision effectively, aligning it with organizational values and goals to rally team members around a shared purpose.

   - Provide leaders with training and support to refine their visioning skills, enabling them to create aspirational goals and inspire others to strive for excellence.

2. **Empowering Others**:

   - Foster a culture of empowerment where leaders delegate authority and decision-making responsibilities to team members, trusting them to take ownership of their work and contribute meaningfully to organizational goals.

   - Equip leaders with coaching and mentoring skills to support the growth and development of their team members, providing guidance, feedback, and encouragement to help individuals unlock their full potential.

3. **Building Trust and Relationships:**

- Emphasize the importance of building trust and fostering positive relationships with team members, stakeholders, and other key stakeholders. Leaders should demonstrate integrity, authenticity, and transparency in their actions, fostering an environment of openness and collaboration.

- Provide leaders with training in interpersonal skills, conflict resolution, and emotional intelligence to enhance their ability to build rapport, resolve conflicts, and cultivate strong relationships built on mutual respect and trust.

4. **Continuous Learning and Development:**

- Promote a culture of continuous learning and development, where leaders are encouraged to seek out opportunities for growth, acquire new knowledge and skills, and stay abreast of emerging trends and best practices in leadership.

- Offer leadership development programs, workshops, and coaching sessions focused on transformational leadership principles, providing leaders with the tools and resources they need to enhance their leadership capabilities.

5. **Innovative Thinking and Risk-Taking:**

- Encourage leaders to embrace innovation and creativity, challenging the status quo and exploring new ideas, approaches, and solutions to organizational challenges.

- Foster a culture that supports experimentation and risk-taking, where leaders are empowered to take calculated risks and learn from both successes and failures.

6. **Recognition and Celebration:**

   - Recognize and celebrate examples of transformational leadership within the organization, highlighting individuals who demonstrate the ability to inspire, motivate, and empower others to achieve extraordinary results.
   - Implement formal recognition programs and informal rituals that acknowledge and appreciate leaders who embody transformational leadership principles and contribute to a culture of innovation and excellence.

7. **Leading by Example:**

   - Encourage leaders to lead by example, embodying the values and behaviors they wish to see in others. Leaders should model authenticity, resilience, and a commitment to continuous improvement, inspiring others to follow their lead.
   - Provide leaders with opportunities to share their own leadership journey and experiences, showcasing the impact of transformational leadership on individual and organizational success.

By implementing these strategies, organizations can effectively cultivate the Transformational Leadership framework in leadership, enabling leaders to inspire, empower, and motivate others to achieve transformative change and drive organizational success.

Transformational Leadership – My Observation and Experience

In my earlier days at Sterling Holidays Resorts, I had the privilege of working closely with a remarkable leader, Oneel, whose approach to leadership left an indelible mark on me. Oneel was not just a leader; he was a visionary, a mentor, and a catalyst for change. His leadership style exemplified the principles of Transformational Leadership, and his impact on the Sales Team and the organization as a whole was profound.

When Oneel took over as the head of Sales, morale was low, and there was a palpable sense of stagnation among the team. The work environment was characterized by complacency and a lack of enthusiasm. However, Oneel saw potential where others saw challenges. He believed in the power of people and their ability to effect positive change.

The first thing Oneel did was to articulate a compelling vision for the future—a vision that inspired and motivated the Sales team to strive for excellence. He painted a picture of what success looked like, emphasizing the importance of innovation, collaboration, and continuous improvement. Through his passionate and visionary communication, he instilled in the team a sense of purpose and direction.

But Oneel didn't just stop at sharing his vision; he actively involved himself in the process of shaping it. He encouraged open dialogue and collaboration, creating a safe space for ideas to be shared and debated. He valued diversity of thought and believed that every team member had something valuable to contribute.

One of the things that struck me most about Oneel was his genuine concern for the well-being and development of his team members. He took the time to get to know each of his team members personally, understanding their strengths, weaknesses, and aspirations. He provided mentorship and support, offering guidance and encouragement whenever needed. He was a true champion of individual growth and empowerment.

Under Oneel's leadership, Sales team underwent a remarkable transformation. Morale soared, creativity flourished, and a culture of excellence took root. Sales Team became more collaborative, innovative, and resilient, tackling challenges head-on and achieving remarkable results.

But perhaps the most significant impact of Oneel's leadership was the lasting impression it left on me. Through his example, I learned invaluable lessons about the power of vision, empowerment, and authenticity in leadership. I saw firsthand how a transformational leader could inspire change, unleash potential, and create a legacy that extended far beyond the confines of the workplace.

As I reflect on my time working with Oneel, I am grateful for the opportunity to have witnessed his transformational leadership in action. His impact on me as a leader and as an individual continues to shape my approach to leadership to this day. And while our paths may have diverged since then, the lessons I learned from him will stay with me forever. Oneel's leadership was not just about achieving results; it was about inspiring greatness in others and leaving a positive and lasting impact on the world.

Conclusion

As we bring our exploration of Transformational Leadership to a close, I find myself reflecting on the profound impact visionary leadership has on organizational dynamics and individual growth. Throughout this chapter, we've delved into the intricacies of Transformational Leadership, uncovering its ability to inspire change, foster innovation, and empower teams toward extraordinary achievements.

Drawing from personal experiences and observations of exemplary leaders, I am deeply moved by the transformative potential inherent in visionary leadership. Whether it's the ability to articulate a compelling vision for the future, empower individuals to action, or cultivate an environment ripe for collaboration and creativity, Transformational Leadership stands as a beacon of inspiration in the corporate landscape.

In today's dynamic and unpredictable business environment, where challenges abound and change is constant, the need for Transformational Leadership is more pertinent than ever. Leaders who embody this framework possess the unique ability to ignite passion, instill purpose, and catalyze progress, not only within their organizations but also in the lives of those they lead.

As we look ahead, let us carry forward the invaluable lessons learned from Transformational Leadership. Let us embrace visionary thinking, cultivate environments of empowerment and growth, and strive to leave a lasting, positive impact on those around us. By embracing the principles of Transformational Leadership, we can unlock the full potential of our teams, organizations, and ourselves, paving the way for a brighter and more promising future for all.

Practical Exercises and Reflection Questions

These exercises and reflection questions are designed to encourage readers to actively apply and critically reflect on the concepts discussed in this chapter. They aim to bridge the gap between theory and practical application, fostering a deeper understanding of how leadership frameworks can be valuable tools in real-world leadership scenarios.

1. **Vision Creating Exercise:**

   - **Exercise:** Take a moment to articulate a vision for your team or organization. What positive changes do you aspire to achieve? Write down your vision statement.

   - **Reflection Questions:**

     ✓ How does your vision inspire and align with the aspirations of your team members?

     ✓ In what ways can you communicate this vision effectively to create a sense of purpose and excitement?

2. **Personalized Leadership Approach:**

   - **Exercise:** Reflect on the individual strengths, needs, and aspirations of your team members. How can you tailor your leadership approach to provide individualized consideration?

   - **Reflection Questions:**

     ✓ What specific actions can you take to support the development and well-being of each team member?

     ✓ How might individualized consideration contribute to a more supportive and engaged team?

3. **Inspirational Storytelling:**

- **Exercise:** Share a personal or organizational story that encapsulates a vision for the future. Consider how storytelling can be a powerful tool for inspirational leadership.

- **Reflection Questions:**

  ✓ How did the storytelling experience impact the engagement and understanding of your audience?

  ✓ In what ways can you integrate storytelling into your leadership communication to inspire and motivate?

4. **Challenging the Status Quo:**

- **Exercise:** Identify a current practice or process within your team or organization. How can you challenge the status quo and encourage creativity and innovation?

- **Reflection Questions:**

  ✓ What potential benefits and risks are associated with challenging the status quo in this context?

  ✓ How can you create an environment that fosters intellectual stimulation and embraces new ideas?

5. **Evaluating Ethical Leadership:**

- **Exercise:** Assess your leadership behaviors against high ethical standards. How do you exemplify idealized influence, and where can improvements be made?

- **Reflection Questions:**

  ✓ In what ways can you further model ethical behavior and build trust with your team?

✓ How might idealized influence contribute to a positive organizational culture?

6. **Cultivating Collective Identity:**

   • **Exercise:** Consider how you can foster a sense of collective identity within your team. What shared values and objectives can unite your team members?
   • **Reflection Questions:**

     ✓ How does a collective identity contribute to a shared commitment to organizational goals?
     ✓ What steps can you take to strengthen the bonds and connections among team members?

7. **Leadership Legacy:**

   • **Exercise:** Envision the long-term impact of your leadership. What legacy do you aspire to leave for your team and organization?
   • **Reflection Questions:**

     ✓ How can your leadership approach contribute to a lasting positive impact on individuals and the organizational culture?
     ✓ What steps can you take today to align your leadership actions with your envisioned legacy?

Chapter 7

Transactional Leadership

In the intricate dance of organizational dynamics, leaders often find themselves balancing the need to inspire and motivate with the necessity to maintain order and achieve results. It is within this delicate equilibrium that Transactional Leadership emerges as a guiding framework, offering a structured approach to setting expectations, driving performance, and navigating the complexities of leadership in today's fast-paced business environment.

In this chapter, we delve into the fundamental principles of Transactional Leadership, exploring how leaders employ rewards and punishments to incentivize desired behaviors, maintain discipline, and achieve organizational goals. From contingent rewards to management-by-exception strategies, we uncover the mechanisms that underpin Transactional Leadership and examine their applications in real-world leadership scenarios.

Join us as we embark on an exploration of Transactional Leadership, unraveling its nuances, and gaining insights into how leaders can leverage this framework to navigate organizational dynamics effectively and drive performance in today's complex and ever-evolving business landscape.

Transactional Dynamics: Emphasizing Exchange for Efficiency

Transactional Exchange Essence

At the core of Transactional Leadership lies a dynamic exchange between leaders and followers. This framework emphasizes a transactional basis, where interactions are akin to a reciprocal agreement. Leaders articulate expectations, set specific goals, and establish a structured system of rewards and consequences based on individual and collective performance. These transactional dynamics forms the bedrock of organizational structure, ensuring that tasks are executed efficiently and align with overarching goals.

Clarity and Efficiency

Transactional Leadership thrives on clarity. Leaders communicate expectations in explicit terms, leaving little room for ambiguity. The exchange of information and directives is precise, creating a structured environment where followers understand their roles and responsibilities. This clarity fosters efficiency, as individuals are guided by well-defined parameters in their pursuit of organizational objectives.

Management by Exception: Navigating Stability

Proactive Stability Maintenance

A pivotal tenet of Transactional Leadership is "management by exception." Leaders intervene or take corrective action only when deviations from established norms occur. This proactive approach to stability maintenance ensures that the organizational ship remains on course. By addressing issues promptly and effectively, leaders prevent minor disruptions from escalating, thereby safeguarding the attainment of organizational goals within predefined parameters.

Clarity and Efficiency

The concept of management by exception implies that leaders focus their intervention efforts selectively. Rather than micromanaging every aspect, leaders target their attention on deviations that have the potential to impact organizational outcomes. This approach acknowledges the autonomy and competence of followers while maintaining a vigilant stance to preserve overall stability.

Transactional Leadership and Employee Motivation

The impact of Transactional Leadership on employee motivation is a crucial aspect to examine, as this leadership style relies on the exchange of rewards and punishments to influence behavior. Here's an analysis of how Transactional Leadership affects individual and team performance, job satisfaction, and organizational commitment:

1. **Individual Performance:**

   Positive Impact:

   Clear Expectations: Transactional leaders set clear expectations and performance standards. This clarity can positively impact individual performance by providing employees with a roadmap for success.

   Reward System: Individuals motivated by rewards may be more likely to meet or exceed performance expectations to receive tangible incentives, such as bonuses, promotions, or recognition.

   Negative Impact:

   Risk of Compliance Over Innovation: Transactional Leadership's focus on conformity to established norms may discourage creativity and innovation. Employees might prioritize meeting predefined expectations rather than exploring new ideas.

Punishments as Deterrents: The use of punishments may create fear, potentially leading to a focus on avoiding negative consequences rather than proactively seeking opportunities for improvement.

2. **Team Performance:**

Positive Impact:

Structured Environment: Transactional Leadership creates a structured environment with clear roles and responsibilities. This structure can contribute to smoother teamwork and coordination.

Aligned Goals: The use of rewards aligns individual and team goals with organizational objectives, fostering a sense of collective purpose.

Negative Impact:

Limited Collaboration: The emphasis on individual goals may hinder collaborative efforts within a team. Team members might prioritize personal rewards over collective success.

Potential for Micromanagement: Leaders practicing active management by exception may be perceived as micromanagers, impacting team autonomy and creativity.

3. **Job Satisfaction:**

Positive Impact:

Rewards as Motivators: Employees motivated by rewards may experience higher job satisfaction when their efforts are recognized and rewarded.

Clear Performance Feedback: Transactional leaders provide feedback through the reward system, which can contribute to a sense of accomplishment and job satisfaction.

Negative Impact:

Punishments and Job Stress: The use of punishments may lead to job stress and dissatisfaction, especially if employees feel constantly under the threat of negative consequences.

Monotony and Routine: The focus on meeting specific targets may result in repetitive tasks, potentially leading to employee boredom and decreased job satisfaction.

4. **Organizational Commitment:**

Positive Impact:

Aligned Values: Transactional leaders can foster organizational commitment by aligning individual and team goals with the values and objectives of the organization.

Recognition and Advancement: Employees motivated by rewards may develop a stronger commitment to the organization when they perceive opportunities for recognition and career advancement.

Negative Impact:

Transactional Exchange Focus: Organizational commitment may be transactional in nature, with employees staying committed as long as the rewards meet their expectations. This commitment might wane if the transactional exchange is perceived as insufficient or unfair.

Limited Emotional Connection: The transactional nature of rewards and punishments may result in a lack of emotional connection to the organization, as commitment is contingent on extrinsic motivators.

In conclusion, Transactional Leadership has both positive and negative impacts on employee motivation, individual and team performance, job satisfaction, and organizational commitment. Leaders must carefully consider the balance between rewards and punishments to create a motivating environment while addressing potential drawbacks associated with a transactional approach.

Fundamental Principles of Transactional Leadership framework

The fundamental principles of Transactional Leadership framework revolve around the concept of exchange and transaction between leaders and followers. Here are the key principles:

1. **Contingent Rewards**: Transactional leaders establish clear expectations and goals for their team members. They offer rewards, such as bonuses, promotions, or recognition, in exchange for meeting or exceeding these expectations. These rewards are contingent upon performance, providing motivation for individuals to achieve their objectives.

2. **Management-by-Exception**: Transactional leaders employ a management-by-exception approach, which involves intervening only when deviations from established standards occur. There are two forms of management-by-exception:

   - *Active Management-by-Exception*: Leaders actively monitor performance and intervene when deviations occur, providing corrective feedback and guidance to maintain alignment with organizational goals.

- *Passive Management-by-Exception*: Leaders intervene only when problems escalate or performance falls below acceptable levels. They maintain a hands-off approach unless issues require their attention.

3. **Clear Expectations and Accountability**: Transactional leaders set clear expectations for their team members regarding performance standards, goals, and responsibilities. They communicate these expectations explicitly and hold individuals accountable for their actions and outcomes. Performance is evaluated based on adherence to established standards, and rewards or consequences are administered accordingly.

4. **Transactional Exchanges**: The relationship between leaders and followers in Transactional Leadership is transactional in nature. Leaders provide rewards or punishments based on the performance of their team members, creating a reciprocal exchange where individuals are motivated to meet expectations in exchange for rewards and to avoid penalties.

5. **Focus on Task Performance**: Transactional Leadership primarily focuses on task-oriented performance. Leaders emphasize achieving specific goals, completing assigned tasks, and meeting performance metrics. The emphasis is on maintaining efficiency, productivity, and adherence to established procedures and standards.

Overall, the fundamental principles of Transactional Leadership revolve around establishing clear expectations, maintaining accountability, and using rewards and punishments to motivate individuals and drive performance within the organization.

Real Life Examples Illustrating Leaders who Exemplify Transactional Leadership Framework

Below are a few real-life examples that showcase how leaders from diverse fields have embodied the principles of Transactional Leadership, inspiring and motivating others to achieve extraordinary outcomes:

1. **Bill Gates – Microsoft:**

   Clear Expectations and Rewards:

   Bill Gates, the co-founder of Microsoft, is often cited as a leader who embraced Transactional Leadership principles. Gates was known for setting clear expectations and linking them directly to rewards. In the early days of Microsoft, he established a performance-driven culture where employees were expected to meet specific targets, and success was rewarded with bonuses and promotions. This transactional approach helped align individual efforts with the company's objectives, fostering a results-oriented environment that contributed to Microsoft's growth and success.

2. **Alan Mulally – Ford Motor Company:**

   Management by Exception:

   Alan Mulally, the former CEO of Ford Motor Company, demonstrated Transactional Leadership through his practice of "management by exception." Mulally implemented a weekly business review meeting where executives provided color-coded status updates. This systematic approach allowed him to identify deviations from the established norms promptly. By intervening selectively and addressing issues as they arose, Mulally maintained stability within the organization. His transactional leadership style played a crucial role in Ford's successful turnaround during a challenging period in the automotive industry.

3. **Sir Alex Ferguson – Manchester United:**

Reward and Punishment Systems:

Sir Alex Ferguson, the legendary football manager of Manchester United, exemplified Transactional Leadership characteristics in the world of sports. Ferguson set clear performance expectations for his players and implemented a system of rewards and consequences. Players who consistently met and exceeded performance standards were rewarded with playing time, contract renewals, and other tangible benefits. On the other hand, Ferguson didn't shy away from employing disciplinary actions, such as fines or exclusion from matches, when players deviated from team norms. This transactional approach helped him maintain discipline, accountability, and a winning culture within the club, contributing to Manchester United's success under his leadership.

What motivates individuals to adopt a Transactional approach to leadership

Individuals may be motivated to adopt a Transactional approach to leadership for several reasons:

1. **Preference for Clarity and Structure**: Transactional Leadership offers a systematic framework characterized by clear expectations, defined roles, and structured processes. Leaders who prefer a methodical approach to leadership, where goals are clearly articulated and progress is measured against predefined criteria, may be drawn to Transactional Leadership. The structured nature of this approach reduces

ambiguity and provides a roadmap for both leaders and team members to follow, enhancing clarity and facilitating effective performance management.

2. **Desire for Results and Accountability**: Transactional Leadership emphasizes achieving specific goals and meeting performance targets. Leaders who prioritize results and accountability, valuing measurable outcomes and tangible achievements, may find Transactional Leadership appealing. By establishing clear performance standards and holding individuals accountable for their actions, leaders can ensure that objectives are met and organizational goals are achieved, driving success and performance improvement within the team or organization.

3. **Preference for Order and Discipline**: Transactional Leadership is characterized by a focus on maintaining order and discipline within the organization. Leaders who value structure, consistency, and adherence to established norms may be motivated to adopt a Transactional approach. The use of management-by-exception strategies allows leaders to intervene when deviations from established standards occur, ensuring that performance issues are addressed promptly and effectively. This approach helps maintain a sense of discipline and control, fostering a productive and efficient work environment.

4. **Belief in Motivation Through Rewards**: Transactional Leadership relies on the use of contingent rewards to motivate individuals and drive performance. Leaders who believe in the power of incentives to inspire action and encourage desired behaviors may be attracted to Transactional Leadership. By offering rewards such as bonuses, promotions, or recognition

in exchange for meeting or exceeding performance expectations, leaders can incentivize individuals to perform at their best and contribute to the achievement of organizational goals. This approach creates a culture of performance and accountability, where individuals are motivated to excel in pursuit of rewards and recognition.

5. **Preference for Transactional Exchanges**: Some leaders naturally gravitate towards transactional exchanges in their interactions with others. They view leadership as a reciprocal relationship, where rewards are offered for desired behaviors and consequences are administered for undesirable actions. Transactional Leadership aligns with this perspective, providing a structured framework for establishing clear expectations, offering rewards for performance, and addressing deviations through corrective action. This approach allows leaders to maintain control and influence outcomes effectively, driving performance and achieving results within the organization.

In summary, individuals may be motivated to adopt a Transactional approach to leadership if they value clarity, structure, results-oriented performance, order, discipline, the use of rewards as a motivational tool, and transactional exchanges in their leadership interactions. Transactional Leadership provides a systematic and effective framework for achieving organizational goals and driving performance improvement, making it a compelling choice for leaders who prioritize accountability, efficiency, and results.

Manifestation of Transformational Leadership framework in day-to-day Leadership practices

The manifestation of Transactional Leadership in day-to-day leadership practices is evident in several key aspects of leadership behavior and interaction. Here's how Transactional Leadership principles translate into practical actions and behaviors:

1. **Setting Clear Expectations**: Transactional leaders establish clear and specific expectations for their team members regarding performance standards, goals, and responsibilities. They communicate these expectations explicitly, ensuring that everyone understands what is required to meet organizational objectives.

2. **Performance Monitoring**: Transactional leaders closely monitor the performance of their team members against established standards and expectations. They track progress, evaluate results, and identify deviations from desired outcomes.

3. **Contingent Rewards**: Transactional leaders use contingent rewards as a motivational tool to reinforce desired behaviors and performance. They offer incentives such as bonuses, promotions, or recognition to individuals who meet or exceed performance expectations.

4. **Management-by-Exception**: Transactional leaders employ management-by-exception strategies to intervene when deviations from established standards occur. They address performance issues promptly, providing corrective feedback and guidance to ensure alignment with organizational goals.

5. **Corrective Action**: Transactional leaders administer consequences, such as reprimands or disciplinary measures, when individuals fail to meet performance expectations or violate organizational norms. They use these corrective actions to maintain accountability and reinforce adherence to established standards.

6. **Goal Alignment**: Transactional leaders ensure that individual and team goals are aligned with organizational objectives. They communicate organizational goals clearly and help individuals understand how their efforts contribute to the overall success of the organization.

7. **Performance Feedback**: Transactional leaders provide regular feedback on performance, highlighting areas of strength and areas for improvement. They offer praise and recognition for achievements and provide constructive criticism and guidance to support development and growth.

8. **Incentive Programs**: Transactional leaders may implement incentive programs or performance-based reward systems to motivate individuals and teams to achieve desired outcomes. These programs may include performance bonuses, sales commissions, or other incentives tied to specific performance metrics.

Overall, the manifestation of Transactional Leadership in day-to-day practices involves setting clear expectations, monitoring performance, using contingent rewards and consequences to drive behavior, and aligning individual efforts with organizational goals. Transactional leaders focus on achieving results, maintaining accountability, and promoting a performance-driven culture within the organization.

Strategies for cultivating Transactional framework in leadership

Cultivating the Transactional Leadership framework involves focusing on the exchange of rewards and incentives for performance, as well as maintaining clear structures and systems to guide organizational operations. Here are strategies for cultivating the Transactional Leadership framework in leadership:

1. **Establish Clear Expectations and Objectives:**

   - Define clear goals, expectations, and performance standards for team members, outlining specific tasks, responsibilities, and deliverables.
   - Communicate expectations transparently and ensure alignment between individual and organizational objectives to provide clarity and direction for team members.

2. **Implement Reward Systems:**

   - Develop and implement reward systems, such as performance-based bonuses, recognition programs, or incentive schemes, to motivate and incentivize team members to achieve desired outcomes.
   - Ensure that rewards are tied directly to performance and align with organizational goals to reinforce desired behaviors and outcomes.

3. **Transactional Leadership Behaviors:**

   - Train leaders to exhibit transactional leadership behaviors, such as contingent reward and management by exception.
   - Encourage leaders to use contingent rewards, such as praise, recognition, or tangible incentives, to reinforce desired behaviors and performance levels.

4. **Performance Monitoring and Feedback:**

   - Establish mechanisms for monitoring and evaluating performance, such as regular performance reviews, progress reports, or key performance indicators (KPIs).

- Provide timely and constructive feedback to team members, highlighting areas of strength and opportunities for improvement, and linking feedback to rewards and recognition.

5. **Clear Communication and Feedback Channels**:

- Foster open communication channels between leaders and team members, ensuring that expectations, objectives, and feedback are communicated clearly and effectively.

- Encourage two-way communication, where team members feel comfortable sharing their ideas, concerns, and feedback with leaders, fostering a culture of trust and transparency.

6. **Adherence to Organizational Policies and Procedures**:

- Reinforce adherence to organizational policies, procedures, and guidelines to ensure consistency, compliance, and accountability within the organization.

- Provide training and support to leaders and team members on organizational policies and procedures, emphasizing the importance of following established protocols and standards.

7. **Performance-Based Development Plans**:

- Develop individualized development plans for team members based on their performance assessments and career aspirations.

- Provide opportunities for skill development, training, and professional growth that are linked to performance outcomes and aligned with organizational objectives.

8. **Recognition of Achievement:**

- Recognize and reward individuals and teams for achieving specific goals, milestones, or targets, reinforcing the connection between performance and rewards.
- Celebrate achievements publicly and acknowledge the contributions of team members to encourage continued performance and motivation.

By implementing these strategies, organizations can effectively cultivate the Transactional Leadership framework in leadership, promoting performance-driven behaviors, accountability, and results-oriented practices within the organization.

Transactional Leadership – My Observation and Experience

In my years of navigating the corporate landscape, I've encountered various leadership styles, each leaving its unique imprint on organizational dynamics. Among them, Transactional Leadership stands out as a pragmatic framework that I've observed firsthand in action.

Allow me to share a story from my own experience, one that vividly illustrates the essence of Transactional Leadership:

During my tenure at a leading home healthcare services firm, One Life, I had the opportunity to work closely with a seasoned leader, Rahul. Rahul was known for his no-nonsense approach to leadership, characterized by clear expectations, structured processes, and a focus on results.

One particular project stands out in my memory. Our team was tasked with launching a new product line, and the stakes were high. As the project unfolded, Rahul's Transactional Leadership style became increasingly apparent.

Firstly, Rahul set clear expectations for each team member, outlining their roles, responsibilities, and performance targets. There was no room for ambiguity; everyone knew what was expected of them.

Secondly, Rahul closely monitored our progress, tracking key performance indicators and intervening when necessary. If someone fell behind schedule or deviated from the established plan, Rahul would step in with corrective feedback and guidance to realign efforts with organizational goals.

But perhaps the most striking aspect of Rahul's leadership style was his use of contingent rewards. As the project progressed, Rahul incentivized high performance by giving recognition to individuals who exceeded their targets. This motivated the team to go above and beyond, knowing that their efforts would be rewarded.

However, Rahul also made it clear that there were consequences for underperformance. Individuals who failed to meet expectations were held accountable through corrective action, whether it be additional training, reassignment of tasks, or other disciplinary measures.

Through Rahul's Transactional Leadership approach, our team successfully launched the new product line on time and within budget. The structured framework he provided, coupled with the use of rewards and consequences, drove performance, maintained accountability, and ultimately led to the project's success.

This experience left a lasting impression on me, highlighting the effectiveness of Transactional Leadership in achieving results and driving performance within organizations. While it may not be the most glamorous or innovative leadership style, Transactional Leadership's pragmatic approach can yield tangible outcomes in the fast-paced world of corporate leadership.

Conclusion

In concluding our exploration of Transactional Leadership, I am reminded of the nuanced balance between structure and motivation that this framework embodies. Through my own observations and experiences, I've witnessed the impactful role that Transactional Leadership plays in driving performance and achieving results within organizations.

Transactional Leadership, with its emphasis on clear expectations, contingent rewards, and management-by-exception, provides a structured approach to leadership that fosters accountability and drives action. In my journey as a leader, I've seen how setting clear goals and providing tangible incentives can motivate individuals to perform at their best and contribute to the success of the team and organization.

However, Transactional Leadership is not without its limitations. While effective in maintaining order and driving short-term performance, it may fall short in fostering creativity, innovation, and long-term growth. As leaders, we must recognize the importance of balancing Transactional Leadership with other leadership approaches, such as Transformational Leadership, to create a dynamic and adaptive organizational culture.

In closing, I believe that Transactional Leadership has a valuable place in the leadership toolkit, offering a pragmatic framework for achieving organizational goals and driving performance. By leveraging its principles judiciously and complementing them with other leadership styles, we can create environments that inspire excellence, foster growth, and drive sustainable success for our teams and organizations.

Practical Exercises and Reflection Questions

These exercises and reflection questions are designed to encourage readers to actively apply and critically reflect on the concepts discussed in this chapter. They aim to bridge the gap between theory and practical application, fostering a deeper understanding of how leadership frameworks can be valuable tools in real-world leadership scenarios.

1. **Performance Alignment Exercise:**

    - **Exercise:** Identify a recent project or team goal within your organization. Clarify and document specific performance expectations for team members.
    - **Reflection Questions:**
        - ✓ How did the clarity of expectations impact the team's performance?
        - ✓ Were there instances where deviations occurred, and how were they addressed?

2. **Setting Reward Systems:**

    - **Exercise:** Design a simple reward system for your team based on achieving specific milestones or goals. Consider both tangible and non-tangible rewards.
    - **Reflection Questions:**
        - ✓ How do you think the introduction of a reward system would influence motivation and performance?
        - ✓ Are there potential challenges or drawbacks to implementing such a system?

3. **Simulated Management by Exception:**

    - **Exercise:** Create a hypothetical scenario where a deviation from established norms occurs. Develop a plan for selective intervention based on the principles of "management by exception."

- **Reflection Questions:**

  - ✓ How would proactive intervention in response to deviations contribute to organizational stability?
  - ✓ What factors would you consider when selectively intervening in such a scenario?

4. **Reflecting on Past Corrections:**

   - **Exercise:** Recall a situation where corrective action was necessary in your leadership experience. Analyze the effectiveness of the correction and its impact on team dynamics.

   - **Reflection Questions:**

     - ✓ How did the correction align with transactional leadership principles?
     - ✓ Were there alternative approaches that could have been more effective?

5. **Team Feedback Session:**

   - **Exercise:** Conduct a feedback session with your team to discuss their perspectives on clarity of expectations, rewards, and consequences.

   - **Reflection Questions:**

     - ✓ What insights did you gain from the team's feedback about the effectiveness of the transactional dynamics?
     - ✓ How might you adjust your leadership approach based on this feedback?

6. **Personalized Reward System:**

- **Exercise:** Reflect on your leadership style and consider implementing a personalized reward system for team members based on their individual strengths and contributions.

- **Reflection Questions:**

  - ✓ How can tailoring rewards to individual team members enhance motivation and engagement?
  - ✓ Are there potential challenges in implementing personalized reward systems?

7. **Scenario Analysis – Balancing Clarity and Flexibility:**

- **Exercise:** Develop scenarios where balancing clarity and flexibility is crucial. Explore how transactional leadership principles can be adapted in dynamic situations.

- **Reflection Questions:**

  - ✓ How can the transactional approach be flexibly applied in scenarios that demand adaptability?
  - ✓ What strategies can enhance clarity without sacrificing flexibility?

Chapter 8

Servant Leadership

In the vast landscape of leadership theories, Servant Leadership stands as a beacon of transformation, offering a paradigm that redefines the very essence of leadership. This introduction sets the stage for a profound exploration of a philosophy that challenges conventional notions of authority and power.

Servant Leadership introduces a fundamental paradigm shift in the traditional understanding of leadership. Rather than viewing leaders as authoritative figures at the top of a hierarchical structure, this concept envisions leaders as servants—individuals dedicated to the well-being and growth of their teams and communities. At its core, Servant Leadership challenges the conventional use of authority and power. Instead of leaders asserting control from a position of dominance, Servant Leadership emphasizes empowerment, collaboration, and the facilitation of others' success. The authority of a servant leader is derived from their commitment to serving the needs of their followers.

Servant Leadership paints a picture of leaders as stewards—custodians of the well-being and development of those under their guidance. This stewardship extends beyond the organizational boundaries to encompass the broader community. Leaders, in this context, see themselves as responsible for fostering a positive impact on both their teams and the society they serve.

Join us as we delve into the heart of Servant Leadership, discovering how this compassionate and altruistic approach can foster collaboration, cultivate trust, and ignite a spirit of collective purpose and fulfillment within teams and organizations. Through real-world examples and practical insights, we delve into the profound philosophy of Servant Leadership, we will also explore how this approach resonates with leaders and transforms organizational cultures. We aim to illuminate the path for leaders who aspire to lead not from a position of power but from a commitment to serving the greater good.

Fundamental Principles of Servant Leadership

Servant Leadership is grounded in a set of fundamental principles that emphasize empathy, humility, and service to others. Here are the key principles of the Servant Leadership framework, elaborated upon:

1. **Servant Heart**: Servant Leaders possess a profound commitment to serving others, rooted in a genuine desire to make a positive difference in the lives of those they lead. They approach leadership as a calling to serve, rather than a position of power or authority. This principle emphasizes the importance of putting the needs of others first and actively seeking opportunities to support and uplift those around them.

2. **Empathy**: Empathy lies at the heart of Servant Leadership, enabling leaders to understand and resonate with the experiences, emotions, and perspectives of their team members. Servant Leaders actively listen to others without judgment, seeking to understand their needs, concerns, and aspirations. By demonstrating empathy, leaders create a sense of psychological safety and trust, fostering open communication and collaboration within the team.

3. **Humility**: Humility is a hallmark trait of Servant Leadership, characterized by a modest and self-effacing attitude. Servant Leaders recognize their own limitations and imperfections, acknowledging that they do not have all the answers and can learn from others. This principle emphasizes the importance of setting aside ego and personal ambition in favor of the collective well-being of the team and organization.

4. **Stewardship**: Servant Leaders view themselves as stewards of their organization's resources, entrusted with the responsibility to manage them wisely and ethically. They prioritize long-term sustainability over short-term gains, making decisions that benefit the organization as a whole rather than serving their own interests. This principle underscores the importance of ethical leadership, integrity, and accountability in guiding organizational decision-making.

5. **Commitment to Growth**: Servant Leaders are deeply committed to the growth and development of their team members. They create environments that foster continuous learning, personal growth, and professional development. Servant Leaders invest time and resources in supporting the growth aspirations of their team members, providing mentorship, coaching, and opportunities for skill-building and advancement.

6. **Building Community**: Servant Leaders recognize the importance of building a sense of community and belonging within their teams and organizations. They foster a culture of inclusivity, trust, and mutual respect, where every individual feels valued, heard, and appreciated. Servant Leaders prioritize collaboration and teamwork, encouraging the sharing of ideas, perspectives, and experiences to achieve common goals.

7. **Lead by Example**: Servant Leaders lead by example, embodying the values and behaviors they wish to see in others. They model integrity, authenticity, and ethical conduct in all their interactions, inspiring trust and confidence in their leadership. Servant Leaders demonstrate a strong work ethic, resilience, and a commitment to excellence, motivating others to strive for their best and contributing to a positive organizational culture.

By embracing these fundamental principles of Servant Leadership, leaders can create environments where individuals feel supported, empowered, and inspired to reach their full potential. Servant Leadership fosters a culture of service, collaboration, and mutual respect, driving organizational success and creating lasting impact in the lives of those they lead.

Profound Impact of Servant Leadership

The profound impact of Servant Leadership extends across various dimensions within organizations, profoundly shaping culture, fostering collaboration, and driving long-term success. Here's a closer exploration of its impact:

1. **Culture of Trust and Empowerment**: Servant Leadership cultivates a culture of trust and empowerment within teams and organizations. By prioritizing the needs of others and demonstrating empathy and humility, Servant Leaders create environments where individuals feel valued, respected, and trusted. This sense of trust empowers team members to take ownership of their work, contribute their unique talents and perspectives, and collaborate effectively towards shared goals.

2. **Enhanced Employee Engagement and Satisfaction**: Servant Leadership fosters high levels of employee engagement

and satisfaction by creating a supportive and inclusive work environment. When leaders prioritize the well-being and growth of their team members, employees feel more motivated, committed, and invested in their work. Servant Leaders empower individuals to develop their skills, pursue meaningful work, and achieve a sense of fulfillment and purpose in their roles.

3. **Improved Communication and Collaboration**: Servant Leadership promotes open communication, transparency, and collaboration among team members. By actively listening to others, valuing diverse perspectives, and fostering a culture of respect and trust, Servant Leaders create opportunities for meaningful dialogue and idea-sharing. This collaborative environment enables teams to innovate, problem-solve, and make informed decisions collectively, driving organizational effectiveness and performance.

4. **Higher Levels of Innovation and Creativity**: Servant Leadership encourages innovation and creativity by creating a safe space for experimentation and risk-taking. When leaders empower their team members to explore new ideas, challenge the status quo, and learn from failure, they inspire a culture of innovation and continuous improvement. Servant Leaders foster a growth mindset, where individuals feel encouraged to stretch beyond their comfort zones, explore new possibilities, and drive positive change within the organization.

5. **Enhanced Organizational Resilience and Adaptability**: Servant Leadership enhances organizational resilience and adaptability by promoting agility, flexibility, and responsiveness to change. When leaders prioritize the well-being of their team members and actively support their

growth and development, they create a workforce that is better equipped to navigate challenges and embrace change. Servant Leaders foster a culture of learning and adaptability, where individuals are empowered to embrace uncertainty, learn from setbacks, and pivot in response to evolving circumstances.

6. **Sustainable Organizational Performance**: Servant Leadership ultimately drives sustainable organizational performance by fostering a culture of service, collaboration, and continuous improvement. When leaders prioritize the needs of others and focus on building strong relationships and trust, they lay the foundation for long-term success. Servant Leaders inspire loyalty, commitment, and dedication among their team members, resulting in higher levels of productivity, innovation, and organizational effectiveness over time.

In summary, Servant Leadership has a profound impact on organizations by shaping culture, fostering collaboration, driving employee engagement and satisfaction, promoting innovation and creativity, enhancing organizational resilience and adaptability, and ultimately driving sustainable organizational performance. By embracing the principles of Servant Leadership, leaders can create environments where individuals thrive, teams excel, and organizations achieve their full potential.

Servants Leadership framework's role in nurturing inclusive and empowering cultures

Servant Leadership framework plays a pivotal role in nurturing inclusive and empowering cultures within organizations, thereby inspiring greatness in others. Here's how:

1. **Valuing Diversity and Inclusion**: Servant Leaders prioritize diversity and inclusion, recognizing the value of diverse

perspectives, backgrounds, and experiences. By fostering an environment where all individuals feel respected, valued, and included, Servant Leaders create a culture of belonging where everyone can contribute their unique talents and perspectives. This inclusive culture encourages collaboration, innovation, and creativity, as individuals from diverse backgrounds come together to solve problems and drive positive change.

2. **Empowering Others**: Servant Leaders empower others by providing them with the support, resources, and opportunities they need to succeed. By delegating authority, trusting their team members, and encouraging autonomy, Servant Leaders enable individuals to take ownership of their work and make meaningful contributions. This empowerment fosters a sense of ownership and accountability among team members, motivating them to strive for excellence and take initiative in their roles.

3. **Fostering Growth and Development**: Servant Leaders prioritize the growth and development of their team members, investing time and resources in their professional and personal growth. By providing mentorship, coaching, and opportunities for learning and advancement, Servant Leaders enable individuals to reach their full potential and achieve greatness in their careers. This focus on growth and development creates a culture of continuous learning and improvement, where individuals are inspired to challenge themselves and pursue excellence in their work.

4. **Leading with Humility**: Servant Leaders lead with humility, recognizing their own limitations and imperfections. By admitting mistakes, seeking feedback, and showing vulnerability, Servant Leaders create an environment where

others feel comfortable doing the same. This humility fosters a culture of openness and honesty, where individuals feel empowered to speak up, share ideas, and collaborate effectively. It also encourages a spirit of mutual respect and appreciation, as team members recognize and value each other's contributions.

5. **Promoting Servant Leadership Among Others**: Servant Leaders inspire greatness in others by modeling servant leadership behaviors and values. By demonstrating empathy, compassion, and a commitment to serving others, Servant Leaders set an example for their team members to follow. They encourage others to embrace the principles of Servant Leadership, empowering them to lead with integrity, compassion, and a focus on the greater good. This ripple effect spreads throughout the organization, inspiring a culture of servant leadership at all levels.

Overall, Servant Leadership framework nurtures inclusive and empowering cultures by valuing diversity and inclusion, empowering others, fostering growth and development, leading with humility, and promoting servant leadership among others. By embodying these principles, Servant Leaders inspire greatness in others and create environments where individuals thrive, teams excel, and organizations achieve their full potential.

What motivates individuals to adopt a service-oriented approach to leadership?

The adoption of a service-oriented approach to leadership, as exemplified by Servant Leadership, is motivated by a range of intrinsic and extrinsic factors. Leaders who embrace this philosophy are driven by a deep understanding of the transformative power of service and the positive impact it can have on individuals, teams, and the broader community.

Here are key motivations for individuals to adopt a service-oriented approach to leadership:

1. **Intrinsic Fulfillment:**

   Purpose and Meaning: Service-oriented leaders are motivated by a sense of purpose and the desire to contribute meaningfully to the well-being of others. They find intrinsic fulfillment in making a positive impact on the lives of their team members and the community.

2. **Empathy and Compassion:**

   Understanding Others: Service-oriented leaders possess a high degree of empathy and compassion. They are genuinely concerned about the needs, feelings, and aspirations of those they lead. This empathy drives them to prioritize the well-being of others.

3. **Building Trust and Collaboration:**

   Fostering Trust: Service-oriented leaders recognize that trust is a foundational element of effective leadership. By prioritizing the needs of their team members, they build trust and create an environment where collaboration and open communication thrive.

4. **Long Term Relationship Building:**

   Investing in People: Servant leaders see leadership as a journey of building long-term relationships. They understand that investing time and effort in the personal and professional growth of individuals leads to stronger, more resilient teams.

5. **Alignment with Organizational Values:**

Organizational Culture: In organizations that value a culture of service and social responsibility, leaders may be motivated to align their leadership approach with these values. Service-oriented leaders contribute to the creation and sustenance of a positive organizational culture.

6. **Recognition of Interconnectedness:**

Global Perspective: Service-oriented leaders recognize the interconnectedness of individuals and communities. They understand that the success of the organization is intertwined with the well-being of its members and the broader society.

7. **Personal Growth and Development:**

Leadership as a Journey: Individuals motivated by personal growth and development are drawn to service-oriented leadership. They see leadership not as a position of authority but as a continuous journey of learning, adapting, and evolving.

8. **Positive Organizational Outcomes:**

Enhancing Performance: Service-oriented leaders understand that focusing on the needs of their team members leads to positive organizational outcomes. By empowering individuals and fostering a supportive culture, they contribute to enhanced performance, innovation, and goal attainment.

9. **Legacy and Impact:**

Leaving a Positive Legacy: Service-oriented leaders are motivated by the desire to leave a positive legacy. They aim to be remembered for the positive impact they made on the lives of individuals and the communities they served.

10. **Alignment with Ethical Principles:**

Ethical Leadership: For some, adopting a service-oriented approach aligns with ethical principles and a commitment to moral leadership. They see service as a fundamental ethical responsibility that guides their decision-making and actions.

In summary, the motivations for adopting a service-oriented approach to leadership are diverse and often rooted in a deep understanding of the holistic impact that leadership can have on individuals and society. It reflects a commitment to a leadership philosophy that prioritizes service as the cornerstone of effective and meaningful leadership.

Manifestation of Servant Leadership framework in day-to-day Leadership practices

The philosophy of Servant Leadership manifests in day-to-day leadership practices through a set of intentional behaviors, attitudes, and actions that prioritize the needs and well-being of others. Leaders who embrace this philosophy seek to serve their team members, foster a positive organizational culture, and contribute to greater good.

Here are ways in which the principles of Servant Leadership manifest in day-to-day leadership practices:

1. **Active Listening:**

Practice: Servant leaders engage in active listening during team interactions.

Impact: By truly understanding the concerns and ideas of team members, leaders demonstrate their commitment to serving their needs.

2. **Empathy and Compassion:**

   Practice: Leaders express empathy and compassion in their interactions.

   Impact: Recognizing and addressing the emotions and challenges of team members creates a supportive and caring work environment.

3. **Putting Others First:**

   Practice: Servant leaders prioritize the needs of their team members.

   Impact: By putting others first, leaders build trust and create a culture where individuals feel valued and supported.

4. **Development and Growth:**

   Practice: Leaders invest in the personal and professional development of team members.

   Impact: Supporting the growth of individuals fosters a sense of fulfillment and loyalty, contributing to long-term success.

5. **Decision Making:**

   Practice: Leaders involve team members in decision-making processes.

   Impact: By seeking input and valuing diverse perspectives, leaders empower their teams and build a collaborative culture.

6. **Recognition and Appreciation:**

   Practice: Leaders actively recognize and appreciate the contributions of team members.

Impact: Acknowledging individual efforts boosts morale, motivation, and a positive team atmosphere.

7. **Conflict Resolution:**

Practice: Leaders approach conflict resolution with a focus on understanding and collaboration.

Impact: Resolving conflicts with empathy and a problem-solving mindset strengthens relationships and team cohesion.

8. **Building Trust:**

Practice: Leaders prioritize building and maintaining trust within the team.

Impact: Trust is the foundation of effective leadership, and leaders who prioritize it create a healthy and resilient team dynamic.

9. **Goal Setting:**

Practice: Leaders collaboratively set goals with team members, aligning individual aspirations with organizational objectives.

Impact: Shared goals and a sense of ownership lead to increased commitment and enthusiasm.

10. **Community Engagement:**

Practice: Servant leaders extend their service-oriented approach beyond the workplace to community engagement.

Impact: By contributing to community well-being, leaders embody the broader impact of Servant Leadership.

11. **Continuous Reflection and Improvement:**

Practice: Servant leaders engage in self-reflection and seek feedback for continuous improvement.

Impact: A commitment to personal growth enhances leadership effectiveness and reinforces the servant leadership philosophy.

In essence, Servant Leadership is not just a theoretical framework but a lived philosophy that permeates the daily actions and decisions of leaders. It is about creating a culture of service, humility, and empowerment that transforms the workplace into a nurturing environment where individuals and teams can thrive.

Real Life Examples Illustrating Leaders who Exemplify Servant Leadership Framework

Below are a few real-life examples that showcase how leaders exemplify servant leadership through their commitment to serving others, fostering inclusivity, and making a positive impact on society. Their influence extends beyond their immediate spheres, inspiring others to adopt a similar ethos of humility, empathy, and a dedication to the greater good.

1. **Mahatma Gandhi:**

Servant Leadership Traits:

- Humility: Gandhi exhibited humility, considering himself a servant of the people rather than a traditional leader.
- Empathy: He deeply empathized with the struggles and needs of the Indian population, advocating for social justice and nonviolent resistance.

- Putting Others First: Gandhi prioritized the well-being of others, leading by example through self-sacrifice and a commitment to nonviolence.

Impact: Gandhi's servant leadership played a pivotal role in India's fight for independence and inspired movements for civil rights and freedom worldwide.

2. **Nelson Mandela:**

Servant Leadership Traits:

- Visionary: Mandela had a vision of a united and democratic South Africa, focusing on reconciliation and equality.
- Empowerment: He empowered others by promoting inclusivity, forgiveness, and collaboration across racial divides.
- Sacrifice: Mandela's willingness to endure imprisonment for the greater good showcased his commitment to serving the needs of the nation.

Impact: Mandela's servant leadership was instrumental in the dismantling of apartheid and the establishment of a democratic, inclusive South Africa.

3. **Mother Teresa:**

Servant Leadership Traits:

- Compassion: Mother Teresa exemplified compassion by dedicating her life to serving the poor and sick.
- Selflessness: She lived a life of selflessness, putting the needs of others before her own comfort or desires.

- Commitment to Others: Mother Teresa's unwavering commitment to alleviating suffering and poverty demonstrated her servant-hearted approach.

Impact: Mother Teresa's servant leadership left a lasting legacy through the humanitarian work of Missionaries of Charity, impacting the lives of countless individuals worldwide.

4. **Herb Kelleher – Co-Founder and Former CEO of Southwest Airlines:**

Servant Leadership Traits:

- Employee-Centric Approach: Kelleher prioritized the well-being of Southwest Airlines employees, recognizing their contributions.
- Approachability: He maintained an approachable leadership style, engaging with employees and fostering a positive workplace culture.
- Putting Employees First: Kelleher's leadership philosophy emphasized that satisfied employees lead to satisfied customers and, ultimately, business success.

Impact: Under Kelleher's servant leadership, Southwest Airlines became known for its exceptional customer service and employee satisfaction, achieving sustained profitability.

Strategies for cultivating Servant leadership framework

Cultivating the Servant Leadership framework involves prioritizing the needs of others, fostering collaboration, and empowering individuals to achieve their full potential. Here are strategies for cultivating the Servant Leadership framework in leadership:

1. **Embrace a Service Mindset:**

   - Encourage leaders to adopt a service-oriented mindset, focusing on meeting the needs of their team members, colleagues, and stakeholders.
   - Foster a culture of empathy, compassion, and humility, where leaders prioritize the well-being and growth of others above their own interests.

2. **Lead by Example:**

   - Model servant leadership behaviors and values in daily interactions and decision-making processes.
   - Demonstrate integrity, authenticity, and servant-heartedness in leadership actions, inspiring others to emulate these qualities.

3. **Develop Listening Skills:**

   - Train leaders to actively listen to the concerns, ideas, and feedback of team members, demonstrating genuine interest and empathy.
   - Create opportunities for leaders to engage in one-on-one conversations, team meetings, and feedback sessions to gather insights and build relationships with their team.

4. **Empower and Delegate:**

   - Empower team members by delegating authority, autonomy, and decision-making responsibilities to them.
   - Provide support, resources, and guidance as needed, while allowing individuals the freedom to take ownership of their work and make meaningful contributions.

5. **Coach and Mentor:**

   - Serve as a coach and mentor to team members, providing guidance, encouragement, and developmental opportunities to support their growth and development.
   - Help individuals identify their strengths, areas for improvement, and career aspirations, and provide tailored support to help them achieve their goals.

6. **Promote Collaboration and Inclusion:**

   - Foster a culture of collaboration, teamwork, and inclusivity, where all team members feel valued, respected, and included.
   - Create opportunities for collaboration, cross-functional partnerships, and knowledge-sharing to leverage diverse perspectives and expertise within the team.

7. **Focus on Personal Development:**

   - Invest in the personal and professional development of team members, providing access to training, coaching, and learning opportunities.
   - Encourage individuals to pursue their passions, interests, and professional goals, and support them in their journey toward continuous growth and improvement.

8. **Serve as a Catalyst for Change:**

   - Champion initiatives and initiatives that promote positive change, innovation, and organizational improvement.
   - Encourage individuals to challenge the status quo, question assumptions, and explore new ideas and approaches to drive meaningful change within the organization.

9. **Practice Gratitude and Recognition:**

- Express appreciation and gratitude for the contributions of team members, recognizing their efforts, achievements, and contributions.
- Celebrate successes, milestones, and accomplishments as a team, fostering a sense of pride, camaraderie, and motivation.

By implementing these strategies, organizations can effectively cultivate the Servant Leadership framework in leadership, fostering a culture of service, collaboration, empowerment, and continuous growth and development.

Servant Leadership – My Observation and Experience

In the competitive world of finance, where bottom lines and quarterly reports often overshadow human connections, I had the privilege of witnessing Servant Leadership in action through the remarkable leadership of my former boss, Manoj.

Manoj was the CFO of India vertical of multinational pest control services company, Rentokil Initial, a position that often came with a reputation for tough decision-making and bottom-line focus. However, Manoj's leadership style was anything but conventional. He believed that true success in finance wasn't just about numbers; it was about the people behind them.

One memorable instance that exemplified Manoj's Servant Leadership occurred during a particularly challenging financial quarter. The company was facing pressure from investors to meet ambitious growth targets, and tensions were running high among the finance team.

Instead of resorting to authoritative measures or placing undue pressure on his team members, Manoj took a different approach. He gathered the team together and, in a transparent and empathetic manner, acknowledged the challenges they were facing. He listened intently to their concerns and frustrations, demonstrating genuine care and understanding for each team member's perspective.

Rather than dictating solutions, Manoj empowered the team to collectively brainstorm ideas and strategies for overcoming the challenges. He encouraged open dialogue and collaboration, ensuring that every voice was heard and valued.

Throughout the process, Manoj made it a priority to support the well-being of his team members. He recognized the stress and pressure they were under and took proactive steps to alleviate it. He organized team-building activities, provided opportunities for professional development, and offered personal support and guidance whenever needed.

As a result of Manoj's Servant Leadership approach, the finance team not only met but exceeded the ambitious targets set by investors. More importantly, they emerged from the experience stronger, more cohesive, and more resilient than ever before. Morale soared, trust flourished, and individuals felt empowered to take ownership of their work and contribute their best efforts.

Manoj's example left a lasting impression on me, challenging my preconceived notions of leadership in the finance industry. Through his servant leadership, Manoj demonstrated that success in finance isn't just about numbers on a spreadsheet; it's about nurturing relationships, empowering individuals, and fostering a culture of trust, collaboration, and excellence. His legacy continues to inspire me in my own journey as a finance professional, reminding me of the profound impact that servant leadership can have in any context.

Conclusion

In the intricate tapestry of leadership philosophies, Servant Leadership emerges as a profound and transformative framework that transcends traditional paradigms. As we conclude our exploration of Servant Leadership, we find ourselves immersed in a philosophy that places service at the heart of effective leadership.

Servant Leadership, as expounded by various theorists and exemplified by inspiring leaders, invites us to reevaluate the fundamental purpose of leadership. It challenges us to shift our focus from hierarchical authority to compassionate stewardship, from self-interest to the well-being of others, and from transactional exchanges to transformative relationships.

The essence of Servant Leadership lies in the commitment to serving others, fostering their growth, and contributing to the broader community. It calls upon leaders to listen actively, empathize deeply, and put the needs of their team members and stakeholders first. Through this servant-hearted approach, leaders create environments where trust flourishes, collaboration thrives, and individuals reach their full potential.

As we reflect on the principles of Servant Leadership, we recognize its enduring impact on the lives of those led and the organizations served. Leaders who embody this philosophy become catalysts for positive change, inspiring a culture of shared values, mutual respect, and a commitment to collective success.

In the footsteps of luminaries like Mahatma Gandhi, Nelson Mandela, Mother Teresa, and contemporary leaders, Servant Leadership beckons us to lead not with the aim of authority or personal gain but with a genuine desire to uplift others. It challenges us to be stewards of a vision that extends beyond immediate goals, embracing a holistic perspective that encompasses the well-being of individuals, organizations, and society at large.

Practical Exercises and Reflection Questions

These exercises and reflection questions are designed to encourage readers to actively apply and critically reflect on the concepts discussed in this chapter. They aim to bridge the gap between theory and practical application, fostering a deeper understanding of how leadership frameworks can be valuable tools in real-world leadership scenarios.

1. **Personal Leadership Assessment:**

   Exercise:

   - Conduct a self-assessment of your leadership style, focusing on aspects such as listening skills, empathy, and commitment to the growth of others.
   - Identify specific areas where you can enhance your servant leadership qualities.

2. **Team Feedback Session:**

   Exercise:

   - Facilitate a feedback session with your team to gain insights into how they perceive your leadership style.
   - Encourage open and honest communication about areas where a servant leadership approach can be strengthened.

3. **Servant Leadership Journal:**

   Exercise:

   - Keep a reflective journal over the next month, documenting instances where you applied servant leadership principles in your interactions.
   - Reflect on the outcomes and the impact on relationships within your team..

4. **Community Service Project:**

Exercise:

- Engage in a community service project or volunteer opportunity to experience firsthand the principles of serving others without expecting anything in return.
- Reflect on how this experience influences your perspective on leadership.

Reflection Questions:

1. How have you demonstrated empathy in your leadership role? Share a specific example and the impact it had on your team or organization.

2. In what ways do you actively listen to the needs and concerns of your team members? How can you improve your listening skills to better understand their perspectives?

3. Consider a challenging leadership situation you've faced. How might a servant leadership approach have influenced the outcome?

4. Reflect on a leader you admire who embodies servant leadership principles. What specific traits or actions make them a servant leader, and how can you incorporate similar qualities into your leadership style?

5. How do you prioritize the growth and development of your team members? Share specific strategies you've employed or plan to implement to foster their professional and personal growth.

6. Think about a recent decision you made as a leader. How did you involve your team in the decision-making process, and

how might a more collaborative approach align with servant leadership?

7. Consider the concept of stewardship in leadership. How do you currently act as a steward for your team or organization, and what additional steps can you take to ensure the well-being of those you lead?

8. Reflect on a time when you faced a challenge or setback as a leader. How did you respond, and what role did resilience and commitment to serving others play in overcoming the challenge?

Chapter 9

Authentic Leadership

In the dynamic landscape of leadership theory, one framework stands out for its emphasis on personal integrity, transparency, and genuine connection: Authentic Leadership. In this chapter, we delve into the essence of Authentic Leadership, exploring how embracing one's true self can profoundly impact individuals, teams, and organizations.

Authentic Leadership is not just about mastering a set of skills or techniques; it's about being true to oneself and leading from the heart. It's about embracing vulnerability, owning one's strengths and weaknesses, and cultivating meaningful relationships built on trust and authenticity.

Throughout this chapter, we will explore the principles of Authentic Leadership, examine its role in fostering trust and engagement, and discuss strategies for cultivating authenticity in leadership. Join me on this journey as we uncover the transformative power of Authentic Leadership and discover how embracing your true self can lead to lasting impact and fulfillment in your leadership journey.

Fundamental Principles of Authentic Leadership

Authentic Leadership is a leadership style that emphasizes the genuine and transparent engagement of leaders with their followers. At its core, Authentic Leadership revolves around being true to oneself, aligning actions with values, and fostering honest and open relationships. This approach encourages leaders to exhibit self-awareness, demonstrate integrity, and create an environment where individuals can thrive authentically.

Key fundamental principles of Authentic Leadership are:

1. **Self-Awareness**: Authentic leaders possess a deep understanding of their values, strengths, weaknesses, and personal beliefs. They engage in continuous self-reflection to gain insights into their motivations and aspirations. This self-awareness enables them to lead with authenticity.

2. **Relational Transparency**: Authentic Leadership emphasizes open and transparent communication. Authentic leaders share information candidly, admit mistakes, and acknowledge vulnerabilities. This transparency builds trust and credibility among followers.

3. **Values-Based Decision Making**: Leaders practicing Authentic Leadership make decisions based on their core values. They align organizational goals with their personal beliefs, ensuring that their actions are consistent with the principles they uphold. This values-based approach guides decision-making processes.

4. **Balanced Processing**: Authentic leaders engage in balanced processing, considering diverse perspectives and soliciting input from team members. They value collaboration and inclusivity, creating an environment where different viewpoints are respected and integrated into decision-making.

5. **Positive Psychological Capital**: Authentic Leadership fosters positive psychological capital in individuals and teams. Leaders inspire optimism, resilience, hope, and efficacy. By

creating a positive and supportive climate, authentic leaders contribute to the well-being and motivation of their followers.

6. **Ethical Conduct**: Ethical behavior is a fundamental aspect of Authentic Leadership. Leaders adhere to high moral and ethical standards, demonstrating integrity and fairness in their actions. This commitment to ethical conduct enhances trust and organizational integrity.

7. **Authenticity in Relationships**: Authentic leaders build genuine and meaningful relationships with their followers. They invest time in understanding the aspirations and concerns of team members, fostering a sense of connection and mutual respect.

8. **Adaptability and Continuous Growth**: Authentic leaders embrace adaptability and a growth mindset. They recognize the need for ongoing personal and professional development and encourage a culture of continuous learning within the organization.

9. **Emotional Intelligence**: Authentic Leadership is closely tied to emotional intelligence. Leaders with high emotional intelligence can navigate and understand their own emotions and those of others. This capability enables them to respond empathetically and effectively to various situations.

10. **Empowering Others**: Authentic leaders empower their followers, enabling them to contribute meaningfully to the organization. They provide autonomy, support personal development, and create opportunities for individuals to showcase their skills and talents.

In summary, Authentic Leadership is a holistic and values-driven approach that places emphasis on self-awareness, transparency, ethical behavior, and genuine relationships. Leaders who embody Authentic Leadership foster a positive organizational culture and contribute to the growth and well-being of both individuals and the collective team.

Theoretical Frameworks for Authentic Leadership

Several theoretical frameworks underpin the concept of Authentic Leadership, providing a foundation for understanding its principles and applications. Here are some key theoretical frameworks associated with Authentic Leadership:

1. **Authentic Leadership Model:** The Authentic Leadership Model, proposed by Bill George, is one of the foundational frameworks in this domain. It emphasizes five core dimensions of authentic leaders: understanding one's purpose, practicing solid values, leading with heart, establishing connected relationships, and demonstrating self-discipline. The model highlights the importance of leaders being genuine, self-aware, and committed to serving others.

2. **Ethical Leadership Theory:** Ethical Leadership Theory aligns closely with Authentic Leadership, emphasizing the moral dimension of leadership. Ethical leaders prioritize ethical decision-making, fairness, and transparency. The theory posits that ethical behavior builds trust and enhances the leader's credibility. Authentic leaders, by virtue of their commitment to personal values and integrity, inherently align with the principles of ethical leadership.

3. **Positive Leadership Theory:** Positive Leadership Theory, often associated with positive psychology, focuses on promoting positive emotions, strengths, and ethical behaviors within organizations. Authentic Leadership is considered a positive leadership approach as it encourages leaders to bring

their authentic selves to work, foster positive relationships, and contribute to a positive organizational culture.

4. **Social Identity Theory:** Social Identity Theory explores how individuals derive a sense of identity and belonging from their social groups. In the context of Authentic Leadership, leaders build a shared identity with their teams based on authenticity and trust. The theory suggests that when leaders express their authentic selves, team members are more likely to identify with the leader and the organization, leading to increased engagement and commitment.

5. **Self Determination Theory:** Self-Determination Theory focuses on understanding human motivation. Authentic Leadership, with its emphasis on individual purpose and values, aligns with SDT by acknowledging the importance of autonomy, competence, and relatedness in motivating individuals. Authentic leaders support the fulfillment of basic psychological needs, fostering intrinsic motivation among team members.

6. **Transformational Leadership Theory:** Transformational Leadership shares commonalities with Authentic Leadership in its focus on inspiring and motivating followers. Both theories emphasize the leader's commitment to values, vision, and ethical conduct. Authentic Leadership, however, places a unique emphasis on the leader's genuine self-expression and self-awareness, distinguishing it from other leadership theories.

7. **Servant Leadership Theory:** Servant Leadership Theory and Authentic Leadership share a commitment to serving others and prioritizing the well-being of followers. Both

emphasize humility, empathy, and ethical decision-making. While Servant Leadership focuses on the leader's role as a servant to others, Authentic Leadership complements this by emphasizing the leader's authenticity and self-awareness.

These theoretical frameworks collectively contribute to the understanding and development of Authentic Leadership. While each theory offers a unique perspective, the integration of multiple frameworks provides a holistic view of how authenticity, ethics, positive relationships, and motivation intersect in the realm of leadership.

Role of Authentic Leadership framework in fostering trust and engagement

Authentic Leadership plays a crucial role in fostering trust and engagement within organizations. Here's how:

1. **Transparency Builds Trust**: Authentic leaders prioritize transparency in their communication and actions. By openly sharing information, thoughts, and intentions, they create an environment of trust where team members feel informed and valued. When leaders are transparent about decisions, challenges, and opportunities, team members are more likely to trust their leadership and feel engaged in the organization's goals.

2. **Authenticity Breeds Authenticity**: Authentic leaders lead by example, demonstrating authenticity in their words and actions. When leaders are genuine, honest, and true to themselves, it encourages authenticity among team members as well. Authenticity breeds authenticity, creating a culture where individuals feel comfortable being themselves and expressing their ideas, concerns, and perspectives openly.

3. **Vulnerability Strengthens Connection**: Authentic leaders are willing to show vulnerability and share their authentic selves with others. When leaders acknowledge their imperfections, admit mistakes, and express vulnerability, it strengthens their connection with team members. Vulnerability fosters empathy, understanding, and compassion, creating deeper relationships built on trust and authenticity.

4. **Alignment with Values Builds Confidence**: Authentic leaders align their actions with their values and principles, even when faced with challenges or pressure to compromise. When leaders demonstrate consistency between their words and actions, it builds confidence and trust among team members. Team members are more likely to feel engaged and committed to the organization's mission when they see their leaders living out the values they espouse.

5. **Empathy Fosters Engagement**: Authentic leaders demonstrate empathy and compassion towards others, understanding their perspectives, needs, and feelings. When leaders show genuine care and concern for the well-being of their team members, it fosters a sense of belonging and engagement. Team members feel valued and supported, leading to higher levels of motivation, satisfaction, and commitment to the organization.

6. **Open Communication Encourages Participation**: Authentic leaders create an environment of open communication where team members feel encouraged to participate, share ideas, and voice their opinions. When leaders listen attentively, validate perspectives, and create space for dialogue, it fosters trust and engagement. Team members feel empowered to

contribute their unique insights and expertise, leading to greater innovation, collaboration, and problem-solving.

Overall, Authentic Leadership fosters trust and engagement by prioritizing transparency, authenticity, vulnerability, empathy, alignment with values, and open communication. When leaders demonstrate these qualities, it creates a culture where individuals feel valued, empowered, and motivated to contribute their best efforts towards shared goals and objectives.

What motivates individuals to adopt Authentic leadership framework?

The adoption of the Authentic Leadership framework is motivated by a combination of intrinsic and extrinsic factors, reflecting a deep commitment to personal and organizational growth. Here are key motivators that drive individuals to embrace the Authentic Leadership approach:

1. **Alignment with Personal Values:** Authentic Leadership encourages leaders to be true to themselves and align their actions with their deeply held values. Individuals who prioritize congruence between their personal values and leadership behaviors find Authentic Leadership appealing. The framework provides a platform for leaders to express their authenticity, fostering a sense of purpose and fulfilment.

2. **Desire for Genuine Connections:** Authentic Leadership places a strong emphasis on relational transparency and building genuine connections with team members. Leaders motivated by a desire for meaningful relationships within the workplace are drawn to this framework. The opportunity to create a culture of openness, trust, and authentic communication serves as a powerful motivator

for those seeking more meaningful connections in their leadership roles.

3. **Commitment to Personal Growth:** Authentic Leadership involves continuous self-awareness and reflection. Individuals with a commitment to personal growth and development see Authentic Leadership as a pathway to enhance their emotional intelligence, interpersonal skills, and overall leadership effectiveness. The framework encourages leaders to embrace feedback, learn from experiences, and evolve as authentic and self-aware individuals.

4. **Building Trust and Credibility:** Trust is a foundational element of Authentic Leadership. Leaders motivated to build trust and credibility within their teams and organizations are drawn to this framework. By demonstrating transparency, honesty, and ethical decision-making, leaders can establish themselves as trustworthy figures, creating a positive and supportive organizational culture.

5. **Enhancing Employee Engagement:** Authentic Leadership has been linked to increased employee engagement and satisfaction. Leaders who prioritize the well-being and growth of their team members understand that Authentic Leadership can contribute to a positive work environment. The framework fosters a sense of belonging, encourages open communication, and empowers employees, ultimately leading to higher levels of engagement and productivity.

6. **Responding to Changing Leadership Expectations:** In a rapidly evolving workplace landscape, there is an increasing expectation for leaders to be authentic and transparent. Individuals who recognize the changing expectations of leadership and the need for more human-centric approaches

are motivated to adopt Authentic Leadership. This framework reflects a contemporary understanding of leadership that resonates with the values of modern workforces.

7. **Long Term Organizational Success:** Authentic Leadership is not only about individual leadership qualities but also about contributing to the long-term success of the organization. Leaders motivated by a commitment to sustainable organizational growth and positive impact are inclined to adopt Authentic Leadership. By cultivating a culture of authenticity, leaders contribute to employee retention, organizational resilience, and overall success.

8. **Ethical Leadership Orientation:** Authentic Leadership places a strong emphasis on internalized moral perspectives and ethical decision-making. Leaders with a strong ethical orientation and a commitment to principled leadership are motivated to adopt this framework. Authentic Leadership provides a structured approach for leaders to navigate ethical dilemmas and make decisions guided by a strong moral compass.

In summary, individuals are motivated to adopt the Authentic Leadership framework when it aligns with their personal values, fosters genuine connections, supports personal growth, builds trust, enhances employee engagement, responds to evolving leadership expectations, contributes to long-term organizational success, and aligns with an ethical leadership orientation. The framework resonates with those seeking a holistic and human-centered approach to leadership.

Manifestation of Authentic Leadership framework in day-to-day Leadership practices

The philosophy of Authentic Leadership manifests in day-to-day leadership practices through a set of behaviors and attitudes that prioritize self-awareness, relational transparency, ethical decision-making, and genuine connections. Here's how this philosophy comes to life in the daily activities of authentic leaders:

1. **Open and Honest Communication:** Authentic leaders prioritize open and honest communication. They share information transparently, providing context for decisions and admitting when they don't have all the answers. This fosters a culture of trust and openness within the team.

2. **Active Listening:** Authentic leaders engage in active listening to understand the perspectives and concerns of their team members. They create a space where individuals feel heard and valued, contributing to stronger relationships and a more inclusive work environment.

3. **Consistent Values Alignment:** Authentic leaders consistently align their actions with their values. In day-to-day decision-making, they ensure that choices reflect their deeply held principles, reinforcing a sense of integrity and trustworthiness.

4. **Admitting Mistakes and Vulnerability:** Authentic leaders acknowledge their mistakes and vulnerabilities. By demonstrating humility, they create an atmosphere that encourages others to be open about their own challenges, fostering a culture of continuous improvement.

5. **Empowering Team Members:** Authentic leaders empower their team members, providing them with autonomy and trusting them to make decisions. This not only enhances individual growth but also contributes to a sense of ownership and accountability within the team.

6. **Fair and Inclusive Decision Making:** Authentic leaders ensure fairness and inclusivity in decision-making. They seek

input from diverse perspectives, considering the impact of decisions on all stakeholders. This approach contributes to a more equitable and collaborative workplace.

7. **Prioritizing Employee Well-Being:** The well-being of team members is a central concern for authentic leaders. They actively support work-life balance, mental health, and personal development, recognizing that a thriving team contributes to overall organizational success.

8. **Continuous Self-Reflection:** Authentic leaders engage in continuous self-reflection. They take the time to assess their leadership style, learn from experiences, and proactively seek opportunities for personal growth. This commitment to self-improvement sets a positive example for the team.

9. **Building Trust through Actions:** Trust is foundational to Authentic Leadership. Leaders build trust by consistently demonstrating reliability, ethical conduct, and a genuine concern for the well-being of their team. Trust-building becomes an ongoing practice, not just an aspirational goal.

10. **Demonstrating Emotional Intelligence:** Authentic leaders exhibit emotional intelligence in their interactions. They are attuned to the emotions of others, respond empathetically, and manage their own emotions effectively. This enhances team dynamics and contributes to a positive work environment.

11. **Cultivating a Positive Organizational Culture:** The day-to-day actions of authentic leaders contribute to the cultivation of a positive organizational culture. This culture is characterized by mutual respect, collaboration, and a shared commitment to the organization's mission and values.

12. **Modeling Ethical Behavior:** Authentic leaders' model ethical behavior in all aspects of their work. Their commitment to ethical conduct sets a standard for the entire organization, reinforcing a culture of integrity and responsible leadership.

In essence, the philosophy of Authentic Leadership manifests in the small, everyday actions and decisions of leaders. It is not just a set of principles to be upheld on occasion but a continuous and lived commitment to leading with authenticity and purpose.

Strategies for cultivating authenticity in leadership

Cultivating authenticity in leadership requires intentional effort and a commitment to self-awareness, transparency, and genuine connection. Here are several strategies that leaders can employ to cultivate authenticity in their leadership:

1. **Self-Reflection**: Take time for regular self-reflection to gain insight into your values, beliefs, strengths, and weaknesses. Reflect on past experiences, successes, and failures, and consider how they have shaped your leadership style. Self-reflection enables you to better understand yourself and align your actions with your authentic self.

2. **Seek Feedback**: Solicit honest feedback from colleagues, team members, mentors, and trusted advisors. Create a safe space for others to provide constructive feedback on your leadership style, communication, and behaviors. Actively listen to their perspectives and use feedback as an opportunity for growth and self-improvement.

3. **Lead with Transparency**: Practice open and transparent communication with your team members. Share your thoughts, feelings, and intentions openly, and be honest

about your strengths, weaknesses, and areas for growth. Transparency builds trust and credibility, creating a foundation for authentic leadership.

4. **Be Vulnerable**: Embrace vulnerability and be willing to show your authentic self to others. Share personal stories, experiences, and challenges with your team members to foster connection and empathy. Vulnerability creates a sense of authenticity and relatability, allowing others to see you as a genuine and approachable leader.

5. **Stay True to Your Values**: Identify your core values and principles, and strive to uphold them in all aspects of your leadership role. Make decisions aligned with your values, even when faced with difficult choices or pressure to compromise. Staying true to your values strengthens your authenticity and integrity as a leader.

6. **Build Genuine Relationships**: Invest time and effort in building genuine relationships with your team members. Get to know them on a personal level, understand their aspirations, and show genuine care and support for their well-being. Authentic relationships foster trust, loyalty, and collaboration within the team.

7. **Lead by Example**: Lead by example and demonstrate authenticity in your actions and behaviors. Model the behaviors you want to see in others, such as honesty, integrity, and empathy. Your authenticity sets the tone for the team and inspires others to be authentic in their own interactions and relationships.

8. **Embrace Imperfection**: Embrace imperfection and recognize that authenticity doesn't mean being flawless. Allow yourself

to make mistakes and show vulnerability, as it humanizes you and makes you more relatable to others. Embracing imperfection creates a culture where mistakes are seen as opportunities for growth and learning.

By implementing these strategies, leaders can cultivate authenticity in their leadership, fostering trust, connection, and engagement within their teams. Authentic leadership creates environments where individuals feel valued, empowered, and inspired to bring their authentic selves to work each day.

Real Life Examples Illustrating Leaders who Exemplify Authentic Leadership Framework

Below are few real-life examples where leaders have left a lasting impact on their respective organizations by embodying Authentic Leadership principles. Their commitment to transparency, ethical decision-making, and fostering positive organizational cultures has not only contributed to organizational success but has also influenced broader conversations about leadership in the business and academic communities.

1. **Bill George – Former CEO of Medtronic:**

Authentic Leadership Traits:

Bill George is known for his authenticity, transparency, and commitment to ethical leadership. He emphasizes the importance of leaders understanding their "True North" — their core values and beliefs that guide their decisions.

Impact on the Organization:

Under George's leadership, Medtronic experienced significant growth, and the company became a global leader in medical technology. His emphasis on values-driven leadership created a culture of innovation and employee engagement. The impact of his leadership is evident in Medtronic's sustained success and its reputation as a socially responsible and ethical company.

2. **Howard Schultz – Former CEO of Starbucks:**

Authentic Leadership Traits:

Howard Schultz demonstrated authenticity by being deeply involved in the day-to-day operations of Starbucks. He was transparent about the company's challenges and communicated openly with employees. Schultz also prioritized social responsibility and ethical business practices.

Impact on the Organization:

Schultz's leadership played a pivotal role in transforming Starbucks into a global coffeehouse chain. His emphasis on creating a "third place" — a comfortable and welcoming environment — contributed to the company's success. Starbucks under Schultz's leadership became known for its commitment to fair trade practices, environmental sustainability, and providing healthcare benefits to employees. The company's positive organizational culture and global expansion reflect Schultz's impact.

3. **Brene Brown – Researcher and Author:**

Authentic Leadership Traits:

Brené Brown is recognized for her authentic and vulnerable communication style. She shares personal stories of struggle and resilience, encouraging others to embrace vulnerability as a source of strength. Her emphasis on courage, empathy, and connection aligns with Authentic Leadership principles.

Impact on the Organization:

While not a traditional organizational leader, Brown's impact on leadership discourse is substantial. Her TED Talks and books, including "Daring Greatly" and "Leadership Manifesto," have influenced leaders across various industries. Brown's teachings on vulnerability and authenticity have sparked conversations about the importance of emotional intelligence, empathy, and human connection in leadership. Her work has contributed to a cultural shift, encouraging leaders to prioritize authenticity and compassion in their leadership styles.

Authentic Leadership – My Observation and Experience

In my early tenure as an Audit Trainee at a CA firm, I had the opportunity to witness Authentic Leadership firsthand in a corporate setting. Allow me to share a story that exemplifies the transformative impact of Authentic Leadership:

During my time working with a large financial services company, I had the privilege of observing the leadership of Mugdha, CEO. Mugdha was known throughout the organization for her genuine authenticity and unwavering commitment to her values.

One particular instance stands out vividly in my memory. The company was navigating a period of significant change, with the introduction of new technologies and shifting market dynamics. Amidst the uncertainty and complexity, Mugdha's leadership shone brightly as a guiding light for the organization.

During a town hall meeting with employees, Mugdha stood before the entire company, addressing them with honesty, transparency, and humility. She didn't sugarcoat the challenges ahead or downplay the difficulties the organization faced. Instead, she spoke openly about the changes taking place, the impact on employees, and the need for adaptation and resilience.

What struck me most about Mugdha's leadership was her authenticity. She didn't try to project an image of infallibility or perfection; instead, she showed vulnerability and humility, admitting her own uncertainties and fears about the future. Her authenticity resonated deeply with employees, fostering a sense of trust, connection, and solidarity throughout the organization.

Throughout the turbulent times that followed, Mugdha remained steadfast in her commitment to her values. She made decisions guided by integrity, fairness, and ethical principles, even when faced with difficult choices or external pressures. Her unwavering dedication to doing what was right, rather than what was easy, earned her the respect and admiration of employees at all levels of the organization.

Under Mugdha's Authentic Leadership, the company weathered the storm of change and emerged stronger and more united than ever before. Morale improved, trust flourished, and employees felt empowered to bring their authentic selves to work each day. Mugdha's leadership had a profound impact on the culture of the organization, creating an environment where individuals felt valued, supported, and inspired to achieve their best.

Through this experience, I gained a newfound appreciation for the power of Authentic Leadership to drive positive change and transformation within organizations. Mugdha's example serves as a testament to the enduring impact of authenticity in leadership, reminding us all of the importance of staying true to ourselves and our values, even in the face of adversity.

In today's fast-paced and ever-changing business world, Authentic Leadership is more important than ever. By embracing authenticity, leaders can create environments where individuals feel valued, empowered, and motivated to bring their best selves to work each day. And in doing so, they can unleash the full potential of their teams and achieve remarkable success together.

Conclusion

In concluding our exploration of the Authentic Leadership framework, we find ourselves standing on the shores of a leadership paradigm that transcends the ordinary—a paradigm that beckons leaders to navigate the complex landscape with authenticity as their guiding compass.

Authentic Leadership, as illuminated through the pages of this chapter, is not merely a set of principles; it is a profound philosophy that resonates with the very essence of effective and impactful leadership. It invites leaders to embark on a journey of self-discovery, encouraging them to peel back the layers of their authentic selves and lead from a place of genuine introspection.

Through the lens of Authentic Leadership, we have witnessed the power of self-awareness, the transformative impact of transparent communication, and the resonance of values-based decision-making. Authentic leaders, as we've explored, not only cultivate positive organizational cultures but also inspire others to unleash their true potential.

As leaders, let us carry the torch of Authentic Leadership forward, recognizing that it is not a destination but an ongoing voyage of self-improvement and relational growth. The journey involves continuous self-reflection, a commitment to ethical conduct, and an unwavering dedication to fostering environments where authenticity can flourish.

In the ever-evolving panorama of leadership theories, Authentic Leadership stands as a timeless and indispensable guide—a philosophy that urges leaders to be not only competent professionals but also authentic human beings. As we embrace the principles of Authentic Leadership, let us, in turn, become beacons of inspiration for those who look to us for guidance and leadership.

Practical Exercises and Reflection Questions

These exercises and reflection questions are designed to encourage readers to actively apply and critically reflect on the concepts discussed in this chapter. They aim to bridge the gap between theory and practical application, fostering a deeper understanding of how leadership frameworks can be valuable tools in real-world leadership scenarios.

Practical Exercises

1. *Values Clarification:*

   Identify your core values. What principles guide your decision-making? Consider how these values align with your leadership practices.

2. *Life Story Reflection:*

   Reflect on key events and experiences in your life that have shaped your leadership style. How have these experiences influenced your authenticity as a leader?

3. *Leadership Legacy Letter:*

   Write a letter to your future self or to those you lead, outlining the legacy you want to leave as an authentic leader. What impact do you aspire to have on others?

4. *360-Degree Feedback:*

   Seek feedback from peers, subordinates, and superiors about your leadership style. How do others perceive your authenticity, and what adjustments could enhance your effectiveness?

5. *Values Alignment Assessment:*

Assess the alignment between your personal values and the values promoted within your organization. Where are there congruencies, and where might there be tensions?

Reflection Questions

1. *Self-Awareness:*

How would you describe your authentic leadership style? In what ways are you self-aware, and how do you ensure alignment between your values and actions?

2. *Vulnerability and Courage:*

Reflect on a situation where you demonstrated vulnerability as a leader. How did it impact your relationship with your team? What did you learn from that experience?

3. *Handling Challenges Authentically:*

Think about a challenging leadership situation you've faced. How did you navigate it authentically? What would you do differently, if anything, in hindsight?

4. *Building Trust:*

Trust is a cornerstone of Authentic Leadership. How do you build and maintain trust with your team? Are there areas where trust could be strengthened?

5. *Feedback and Growth:*

How do you actively seek and respond to feedback? In what ways do you foster a culture of continuous improvement and personal growth within your team?

6. *Balancing Stakeholders Interest:*

   Consider the various stakeholders you interact with as a leader (employees, customers, shareholders). How do you balance their interests while staying true to your values?

7. *Integrating Authentic Leadership into Decision Making:*

   Reflect on a recent decision you made as a leader. How did your authenticity and values play a role in the decision-making process? What were the outcomes?

8. *Impact on Organizational Culture:*

   Assess the impact of your leadership on the organizational culture. How does your authenticity contribute to a positive and inclusive workplace environment?

Chapter 10

Situational Leadership

In the intricate tapestry of leadership theories, Situational Leadership stands out as a versatile and adaptive framework, acknowledging the dynamic nature of organizational environments. Unlike rigid, one-size-fits-all approaches, Situational Leadership recognizes that effective leadership is contingent upon the nuanced demands of diverse situations. In today's rapidly evolving business landscape, leaders are confronted with a myriad of challenges, from shifting market trends to changing organizational dynamics. Situational Leadership offers a roadmap for navigating these complexities by emphasizing the importance of tailoring leadership strategies to the specific needs of individuals and situations.

Throughout this chapter, we will explore the core principles of Situational Leadership, examine its practical applications in various contexts, and discuss strategies for effectively applying this framework in real-world scenarios. Join me as we unravel the complexities of Situational Leadership and discover how it can empower leaders to thrive amidst uncertainty and change.

Fundamental Principles of Situational Leadership

The Situational Leadership framework is grounded in several fundamental principles that guide leaders in adapting their approach based on the specific needs of their team members and the situational context. Let's delve into these principles:

1. **Contingency and Flexibility:** Situational Leadership thrives on the principle of contingency, understanding that leadership effectiveness is not a static concept but contingent upon the unique demands of each situation. This foundational element emphasizes the need for leaders to be flexible, agile, and ready to adjust their leadership approaches based on the ever-changing dynamics within their teams and organizations. Flexibility allows leaders to effectively navigate the complexities of leadership and achieve optimal outcomes.

2. **Assessment:** Effective Situational Leadership begins with a thorough assessment of the situation and the capabilities of team members. Leaders must accurately diagnose the readiness and competence level of each individual to determine the appropriate leadership style to employ. This assessment serves as the foundation for guiding leadership actions.

3. **Matching Leadership Style to Development Level:** Situational Leadership categorizes team members into different development levels based on their competence and commitment. Leaders then match their leadership style to the specific development level of each individual. This ensures that leadership actions are tailored to meet the unique needs of team members at different stages of their development.

4. **Adaptability:** Situational Leadership recognizes that effective leadership is not a one-size-fits-all approach. Leaders must be adaptable and responsive to changes in the situation and the needs of their team members. This may require shifting

leadership styles or strategies to address evolving challenges and opportunities.

5. **Clarity and Communication:** Clear communication is essential in Situational Leadership. Leaders must clearly articulate expectations, goals, and performance standards to team members, providing them with the guidance and support they need to succeed. Open communication channels foster trust, collaboration, and alignment within the team.

6. **Development and Empowerment**: Situational Leadership aims to develop and empower team members to reach their full potential. Leaders provide support, guidance, and resources to help individuals grow and develop their skills and capabilities. By empowering team members to take ownership of their work and decisions, leaders foster a culture of accountability and self-reliance.

7. **Continuous Assessment and Adjustment:** Situational Leadership is an ongoing process that requires continuous assessment and adjustment. Leaders must regularly evaluate the effectiveness of their leadership approach and make adjustments as needed based on changes in the situation or the development level of team members. This iterative process ensures that leadership actions remain aligned with the needs of the team and the goals of the organization.

In essence, the principles that underpin Situational Leadership's adaptability and resilience in the face of change provide leaders with a robust framework for navigating the complexities of leadership. The recognition of contingency, the understanding of developmental levels, the adaptability in leadership styles, and the focus on continuous learning collectively empower leaders to thrive amid the ever-changing dynamics of organizational life. Situational Leadership, as illuminated by these fundamental principles, is not merely a theory but a dynamic guide for leaders navigating the intricate challenges of change and adaptation.

Theoretical Frameworks for Situational Leadership

Several theoretical frameworks underpin the concept of Situational Leadership, providing a foundation for understanding its principles and applications. These theoretical frameworks provide leaders with conceptual tools for understanding and navigating different situational contexts. By considering factors such as follower readiness, decision requirements, task characteristics, and the quality of leader-follower relationships, leaders can adapt their approaches and enhance their effectiveness in various situations.

Here are some key theoretical frameworks associated with Situational Leadership:

1. **Hersey and Blanchard's Situational Leadership Model:**

   Developed by Paul Hersey and Ken Blanchard, this model is a foundational framework for Situational Leadership. It categorizes leadership styles into four types: telling, selling, participating, and delegating. The model suggests that the most effective leadership style depends on the readiness or developmental level of followers, considering both their competence and commitment. Leaders using this framework can diagnose the developmental level of their team members and adapt their leadership style accordingly.

2. **Vroom-Yetton-Jago Decision-Making Model:**

   This model, initially proposed by Victor Vroom and Phillip Yetton and later refined by Vroom and Jago, focuses on decision-making styles in leadership. It emphasizes the situational aspect of leadership by suggesting that the most effective decision-making style depends on the nature of the decision and the degree of follower input required. The model helps leaders determine whether to make decisions independently, consult with followers, or involve them in the decision-making process.

3. **Path-Goal Theory:**

Developed by Robert House, the Path-Goal Theory is a situational leadership framework that focuses on the leader's role in facilitating the achievement of followers' goals. The theory suggests that leaders should adopt different leadership styles based on the characteristics of the task and the followers. For example, if followers are facing obstacles, a leader may need to be more directive. If tasks are challenging but achievable, a supportive leadership style may be more appropriate.

4. **Fiedler's Contingency Model:**

Fred Fiedler's Contingency Model is another framework that aligns with situational leadership principles. The model proposes that the effectiveness of a leader is contingent upon the match between the leader's style and the favorability of the situation. Fiedler identified two leadership styles: task-oriented and relationship-oriented. The appropriate style depends on factors such as the leader's relationship with followers, the structure of tasks, and the leader's position power.

5. **Cognitive Resource Theory:**

Cognitive Resource Theory, developed by Fred Fiedler and Joe Garcia, is an extension of Fiedler's Contingency Model.

It adds the dimension of cognitive abilities to the situational equation. The theory suggests that in high-stress situations, leaders with higher cognitive abilities are more effective, while in low-stress situations, leaders with lower cognitive abilities can be equally effective. This situational consideration is essential for leaders aiming to adapt their approaches based on the cognitive demands of the situation.

6. **Blake and Mouton's Managerial Grid:**

The Managerial Grid, developed by Robert Blake and Jane Mouton, is a situational leadership framework that assesses leadership styles based on two dimensions: concern for people and concern for production. The model identifies five different leadership styles, ranging from impoverished management (low concern for people and production) to team management (high concern for both). Leaders using this framework can adapt their styles based on the specific needs of the team and the task at hand.

What motivates individuals to adopt a Situational-oriented approach to leadership?

In essence, individuals are motivated to adopt the Situational Leadership framework when they seek a dynamic, adaptable approach that aligns with the challenges of a rapidly changing environment. The framework's focus on personalized leadership, enhanced communication, and continuous learning resonates with leaders who aspire to navigate complexity, optimize team performance, and foster individual and organizational growth.

Here are key motivations for individuals to adopt a situational-oriented approach to leadership:

1. **Effective Response to Change:** The dynamic and adaptable nature of Situational Leadership makes it an appealing framework for individuals motivated to navigate change effectively. In rapidly evolving environments, leaders who embrace Situational Leadership can respond appropriately to shifting circumstances, demonstrating agility, and ensuring the continued success of their teams.

2. **Tailored Leadership Approaches:** Situational Leadership offers leaders the ability to tailor their approaches based on the specific needs and developmental levels of their team members. Leaders motivated by a desire to connect with their team on an individual level find this framework attractive. The personalization of leadership styles fosters stronger relationships and contributes to higher levels of engagement and performance.

3. **Increased Leadership Effectiveness:** The focus on matching leadership styles to the competence and commitment levels of followers is a motivating factor for individuals seeking increased leadership effectiveness. Leaders adopting Situational Leadership can enhance their ability to guide teams successfully through various situations, ultimately achieving better outcomes and organizational success.

4. **Versatility in Leadership Styles:** Motivated leaders appreciate the versatility offered by Situational Leadership. This framework allows leaders to move seamlessly between directive, coaching, supporting, and delegating styles based on the demands of the situation. For individuals motivated to develop a well-rounded leadership skill set, Situational Leadership provides a comprehensive approach that can be adapted to diverse scenarios.

5. **Enhanced Team Performance:** Leaders motivated by a desire to optimize team performance are drawn to Situational Leadership. By adjusting leadership styles to match the needs of individual team members, leaders can create an environment that maximizes each member's potential. This, in turn, contributes to a more cohesive and high-performing team.

6. **Adaptive Leadership Mindset:** Individuals with a motivation for continuous learning and adaptability are likely to be attracted to Situational Leadership. This framework promotes an adaptive mindset, encouraging leaders to continually assess and adjust their approaches. Leaders who value ongoing development and are motivated to stay ahead of the curve find Situational Leadership aligning with their growth-oriented mindset.

7. **Improved Communication Skills:** Situational Leadership places a strong emphasis on effective communication, motivating leaders to hone their communication skills. Leaders adopting this framework actively seek to communicate expectations, provide guidance, and motivate their teams based on the situational context. Enhanced communication contributes to clearer expectations, reduced misunderstandings, and improved overall team dynamics.

8. **Recognition of Individual Development:** Leaders motivated by a commitment to individual and team development find Situational Leadership appealing. This framework recognizes the unique developmental levels of team members and encourages leaders to invest in the growth and advancement of each individual. Motivated leaders

appreciate the impact of tailored development efforts on both individual and collective success.

Manifestation of Situational Leadership in Day-to-Day Leadership Practices

Situational Leadership manifests in day-to-day practices through a dynamic, context-specific, and flexible approach. Leaders actively adapt their leadership styles, communicate effectively, and prioritize the unique needs of individual team members, fostering an environment that is conducive to both individual and collective success.

1. **Assessment of Situational Context:** Leaders practicing Situational Leadership begin their day by assessing the situational context. This involves considering the specific challenges, goals, and the developmental levels of team members. The daily assessment guides leaders in determining the most suitable leadership style for each situation.

2. **Customized Communication:** Effective communication is a hallmark of Situational Leadership. Leaders tailor their communication styles based on the needs of individual team members. This may involve providing clear instructions for tasks requiring more direction or engaging in open dialogues to encourage collaboration and participation in decision-making.

3. **Flexibility in Leadership Styles:** Throughout the day, leaders employing Situational Leadership remain flexible in their leadership styles. They adapt their approaches based on the competence and commitment levels of team members. For tasks requiring specific guidance, leaders may adopt a more directive style, while for projects where team members are highly skilled, a delegative style might be more appropriate.

4. **Individualized Coaching Sessions:** Leaders invest time in individualized coaching sessions to support the development of team members. These sessions focus on addressing specific needs, providing constructive feedback, and offering guidance tailored to the developmental levels of each team member. The goal is to enhance individual capabilities and contribute to overall team success.

5. **Supportive Leadership Presence:** Situational leaders maintain a supportive presence, particularly during challenging situations. They actively engage with team members, offering assistance and encouragement when needed. This supportive approach fosters a positive team environment and demonstrates leadership responsiveness to the emotional and developmental needs of the team.

6. **Delegation based on Competence:** In instances where team members demonstrate high competence and commitment, leaders practicing Situational Leadership delegate responsibilities accordingly. Delegative leadership allows team members to take ownership of tasks, fostering a sense of empowerment and accountability.

7. **Task – Oriented Leadership for Clarity:** Situational leaders may adopt a more task-oriented approach when clarity is crucial. This involves providing explicit instructions, setting clear expectations, and ensuring that team members understand their roles and responsibilities. This practice contributes to streamlined workflows and minimizes misunderstandings.

8. **Adaptation to Changing Dynamics:** Throughout the day, leaders remain vigilant to changing dynamics within the team

and the broader organizational context. They are prepared to adapt their leadership styles in response to unforeseen challenges, emerging opportunities, or shifts in team dynamics. This adaptability ensures that leadership practices remain relevant and effective.

9. **Continuous Learning and Reflection:** Situational leaders prioritize continuous learning and reflection. At the end of each day, they review the outcomes of their leadership approaches, considering what worked well and areas for improvement. This reflective practice contributes to ongoing refinement of leadership skills and the ability to navigate future situations more effectively.

10. **Promotion of Team Collaboration:** The manifestation of Situational Leadership includes promoting team collaboration. Leaders encourage open communication, facilitate teamwork, and create an environment where team members feel comfortable sharing their perspectives. This collaborative approach aligns with the situational context and enhances overall team performance.

Real Life Examples Illustrating Leaders who Exemplify Situational Leadership Framework

Below are a few real-life examples where leaders have left a lasting impact on their respective organizations by embodying Situational Leadership principles. These real-life examples underscore how leaders who embrace the principles of Situational Leadership can have a profound impact on their organizations and societies. By adjusting their leadership styles based on the unique demands of different situations, these leaders effectively navigated challenges, inspired positive change, and left a legacy.

1. **Nelson Mandela:**

Situational Leadership Style:

Nelson Mandela's leadership during the anti-apartheid movement and his presidency in South Africa showcased a dynamic situational leadership style. Early in his career, Mandela adopted a collaborative and diplomatic approach, engaging in negotiations with the apartheid government. However, as the political landscape shifted and reconciliation became a priority, Mandela demonstrated inclusivity, emphasizing unity and forgiveness.

Impact:

Mandela's ability to adapt his leadership style played a pivotal role in the successful transition from apartheid to a democratic South Africa. By embracing a collaborative and inclusive stance during the reconciliation process, Mandela contributed to building a foundation for a more unified and tolerant society. His situational leadership was instrumental in navigating the complexities of post-apartheid governance and fostering a sense of collective identity.

2. **Mary Barra – General Motors:**

Situational Leadership Style:

Mary Barra, as the CEO of General Motors, exhibited a situational leadership style characterized by adaptability to the challenges of the automotive industry. Facing rapid technological advancements, market shifts, and organizational transformations, Barra embraced a flexible leadership approach. She combined a visionary outlook with agility in responding to dynamic industry changes.

Impact:

Barra's situational leadership has been critical in guiding General Motors through transformative phases. Her strategic vision and adaptability to technological shifts, such as the focus on electric vehicles and autonomous technology, have positioned the company as an industry leader. The impact of her situational leadership is evident in General Motors' continued relevance and strategic positioning in the rapidly evolving automotive landscape.

3. **Jacinda Ardern – Former New Zealand Prime Minister:**

Situational Leadership Style:

Jacinda Ardern, as the Prime Minister of New Zealand, demonstrated situational leadership during crises, including the Christchurch Mosque shootings and the COVID-19 pandemic. Her leadership style combined empathy, decisiveness, and collaboration. Ardern adapted her approach to address the specific challenges faced by the nation, showcasing a responsive and situationally aware leadership style.

Impact:

Ardern's situational leadership garnered international praise, particularly during the COVID-19 pandemic. Her swift and decisive actions, transparent communication, and empathetic approach contributed to New Zealand's successful management of the crisis. Ardern's ability to adapt to the unique challenges of each situation showcased her resilience and fostered a sense of national unity, highlighting the impact of situational leadership in times of adversity.

Strategies for cultivating Situational Leadership framework

Cultivating Situational Leadership involves developing a nuanced understanding of the framework's principles and applying them effectively in practice. Here are some strategies for cultivating Situational Leadership:

1. **Develop Self-Awareness**: Effective Situational Leadership begins with self-awareness. Leaders must understand their own leadership style, strengths, and areas for growth. Reflect on your preferred leadership approach and assess how it aligns with the principles of Situational Leadership. Identify areas where you can adapt and evolve your leadership style to better meet the needs of your team members and the situation.

2. **Learn to Diagnose Development Levels**: Master the skill of diagnosing the development levels of your team members. This involves assessing their competence and commitment in relation to specific tasks or goals. Invest time in observing and interacting with team members to gain insights into their capabilities, motivations, and readiness to take on new challenges. Develop a keen eye for identifying the developmental needs of individuals and tailoring your leadership approach accordingly.

3. **Practice Flexibility**: Cultivate flexibility in your leadership approach. Recognize that there is no one-size-fits-all solution to leadership and that different situations may require different approaches. Practice adapting your leadership style to suit the specific needs of your team members and the demands of the situation. Be willing to shift gears, try new strategies, and experiment with different approaches to leadership as needed.

4. **Build Strong Communication Skills**: Effective communication is essential in Situational Leadership. Develop strong communication skills to clearly articulate expectations, goals, and performance standards to your team members. Foster open and honest dialogue, encourage feedback, and listen actively to the concerns and perspectives of others. Clear communication builds trust, alignment, and understanding within the team, enabling you to effectively guide and support team members in their development.

5. **Provide Targeted Support and Guidance**: Tailor your support and guidance to the specific needs of each team member. Provide targeted coaching, mentoring, and resources to help individuals develop their skills and overcome challenges. Offer constructive feedback and praise for progress and achievements and be available to answer questions and provide guidance when needed. By providing personalized support, you empower team members to grow and succeed in their roles.

6. **Empower Team Members**: Foster a culture of empowerment within your team by delegating authority, autonomy, and decision-making responsibility. Encourage team members to take ownership of their work, set goals, and pursue opportunities for growth and development. Create an environment where individuals feel empowered to make decisions, take risks, and learn from their experiences. Empowered team members are more engaged, motivated, and committed to achieving success.

7. **Continuously Learn and Adapt**: Cultivate a growth mindset and a commitment to continuous learning and improvement. Stay abreast of developments in Situational Leadership theory

and practice, and seek out opportunities for professional development and training. Be open to feedback and constructive criticism and use it as a catalyst for growth and self-improvement. Continuously learn from your experiences, adapt your leadership approach accordingly, and strive to become a more effective Situational Leader over time.

By implementing these strategies, leaders can cultivate Situational Leadership skills and effectively apply the framework to navigate the complexities of leadership and drive success within their teams and organizations.

Situational Leadership – My Observation and Experience

In my early career role as a Consultant, I had the opportunity to observe a remarkable display of Situational Leadership within a corporate setting. The story I'm about to share vividly illustrates the principles of this framework in action.

At a technology firm undergoing a major organizational restructuring, I witnessed the leadership of a senior manager, Mohit. Mohit was tasked with leading a diverse team of engineers through a challenging transition period, where new processes and technologies were being introduced.

Early on, Mohit recognized the need to adapt his leadership style to the varying levels of readiness and competence among team members. Some engineers were seasoned veterans familiar with the company's legacy systems, while others were new hires with little experience in the industry.

With this understanding, Mohit adopted a Situational Leadership approach, tailoring his leadership style to match the development level of each team member. For the more experienced engineers who were resistant to change, Mohit employed a supportive and coaching approach. He took the time to listen to their concerns, address their questions, and provide guidance on navigating the transition. He also offered additional training and resources to help them upskill and adapt to the new processes.

For the newer team members who were eager to learn but lacked experience, Mohit adopted a more directive approach. He provided clear instructions, set specific goals and expectations, and closely monitored their progress. He also paired them with more experienced colleagues who could serve as mentors and provide additional support as needed.

As the transition progressed, Mohit continued to assess the development levels of his team members and adjust his leadership approach accordingly. He remained flexible and responsive to their evolving needs, providing the right level of support and guidance at each stage of the process.

Through Mohit's Situational Leadership, the team successfully navigated the organizational restructuring and emerged stronger and more cohesive than before. Morale improved, productivity increased, and team members felt empowered and supported in their roles.

This experience highlighted the transformative power of Situational Leadership in driving organizational success. By adapting his leadership style to meet the specific needs of his team members and the demands of the situation, Mohit was able to effectively lead his team through a period of significant change and achieve remarkable results.

As I reflect on this experience, I am reminded of the importance of flexibility, adaptability, and empathy in leadership. Situational Leadership provides a valuable framework for navigating the complexities of leadership and empowering teams to thrive in dynamic and uncertain environments.

Conclusion

In the realm of leadership theories, the Situational Leadership framework emerges as a beacon of adaptability and responsiveness. As we conclude our exploration of Situational Leadership in this chapter, it becomes evident that effective leadership is not a one-size-fits-all endeavor; rather, it is a dynamic interplay between the leader's actions and the ever-changing contexts in which they operate.

Situational Leadership, pioneered by scholars such as Paul Hersey and Ken Blanchard, underscores the significance of tailoring leadership approaches to the unique needs, readiness, and developmental levels of followers. This adaptive philosophy recognizes that what works in one situation may not necessarily be effective in another. Leaders who grasp the essence of Situational Leadership navigate the complex landscape of organizational challenges with finesse, drawing on a versatile toolkit of leadership styles.

The real-life examples provided in this chapter illuminate the diverse applications of Situational Leadership across different domains. From the political arena with leaders like Nelson Mandela, who adeptly guided a nation through tumultuous times, to corporate landscapes where figures like Mary Barra orchestrated transformations in the automotive industry, and to crisis management exemplified by Jacinda Ardern's decisive leadership during the COVID-19 pandemic – these examples underscore the universal relevance of Situational Leadership.

The impact of Situational Leadership is not confined to specific industries or contexts; rather, it resonates with the core principles of understanding, adapting, and influencing effectively. Leaders who embrace this framework position themselves as agile navigators, capable of steering their organizations through a myriad of challenges while fostering a dynamic and engaged followership.

As we conclude this chapter, the enduring lesson of Situational Leadership is clear: leadership is a journey of continuous adaptation and learning. The leader's ability to assess, adjust, and align their actions with the ever-shifting dynamics of the environment is what sets apart those who merely lead from those who lead with impact. In the chapters to come, we will continue our exploration of leadership frameworks, each offering unique perspectives and insights for the aspiring and seasoned leaders alike.

Practical Exercises and Reflection Questions

These exercises and reflection questions are designed to encourage readers to actively apply and critically reflect on the concepts discussed in this chapter. They aim to bridge the gap between theory and practical application, fostering a deeper understanding of how leadership frameworks can be valuable tools in real-world leadership scenarios.

1. **Situational Analysis:**

    Reflect on a recent leadership challenge you faced. Identify the specific context, including the nature of the challenge, the readiness of your team, and external factors. Analyze how your leadership approach aligned with the situational demands.

2. **Leadership Style Inventory:**

    Conduct a personal inventory of your default leadership style. Consider how often you adapt your style based on the needs of your team and the situation. Identify situations where you tend to be more directive, supportive, participative, or delegative.

3. **Case Study Application:**

    Explore case studies or scenarios where leaders faced distinct challenges. Apply the principles of Situational Leadership to analyze how different leadership styles could have been more effective in those situations. Consider the impact of adjusting leadership approaches.

4. **Team readiness Assessment:**

    Evaluate the readiness levels of your team members for various tasks. Use a readiness assessment tool to categorize tasks based on the competence and commitment of team members.

Reflect on how your leadership style aligns with the readiness levels of your team.

5. **Adaptability Action Plan:**

Develop a plan to enhance your adaptability as a leader. Identify specific actions you can take to adjust your leadership style based on situational demands. Implement this plan and assess the outcomes in terms of team performance and satisfaction.

6. **Peer Feedback Session:**

Engage in a feedback session with peers or team members. Seek input on your leadership style and its effectiveness in different situations. Use this feedback to identify areas for improvement and potential adjustments to your approach.

Reflection Questions

1. Can you recall a situation where your leadership style was particularly effective? What aspects of that situation allowed your approach to be successful?

2. Think about a time when your leadership approach did not yield the desired outcomes. What situational factors might have contributed to the effectiveness or ineffectiveness of your leadership style?

3. In what ways do you currently assess the readiness levels of your team members for specific tasks? How might a more intentional consideration of readiness inform your leadership decisions?

4. Consider a project or task that your team is currently undertaking. How would you categorize the readiness levels of

your team members, and what adjustments to your leadership style might be beneficial?

5. Reflect on your team's feedback regarding your leadership style. Are there consistent patterns in their observations? How might you leverage this feedback to enhance your situational leadership approach?

6. Imagine a future challenge or change in your organization. How could the principles of Situational Leadership guide your approach to effectively lead your team through that situation?

Chapter 11

Charismatic Leadership

Charismatic Leadership is a leadership style characterized by a leader's ability to inspire and captivate followers through extraordinary charm, self-confidence, and a compelling vision. Charismatic leaders possess a magnetic personality that goes beyond conventional authority, drawing people to them through a powerful aura of influence. Central to this leadership style is the leader's capacity to communicate with exceptional clarity, passion, and persuasiveness, creating an emotional connection with followers.

In this chapter, we explore the dynamic and captivating world of Charismatic Leadership. Charismatic Leadership is characterized by the ability to inspire and influence others through powerful vision, compelling communication, and magnetic personality.

In today's rapidly changing and highly competitive business environment, the need for visionary and inspirational leaders has never been greater. Charismatic leaders possess a unique ability to rally individuals around a shared vision, ignite passion and enthusiasm, and drive organizational success through their sheer force of personality.

Throughout this chapter, we will delve into the principles and practices of Charismatic Leadership, examining the traits and behaviors that define charismatic leaders and exploring the impact they have on individuals, teams, and organizations. Join me as we uncover the essence of Charismatic Leadership and discover how it can empower leaders to inspire greatness and achieve extraordinary results.

Fundamental Principles of Charismatic Leadership

Within the dynamic landscape of leadership theories, Charismatic Leadership stands as a beacon of inspiration, captivating hearts and minds with its compelling vision and magnetic influence. At its essence, Charismatic Leadership embodies the art of inspiring and mobilizing others through the sheer force of one's personality and vision. It transcends conventional leadership paradigms, compelling individuals to rally around a shared purpose and pursue collective aspirations with unwavering passion and commitment. As we embark on this enlightening journey, we delve into the fundamental principles that underpin the phenomenon of Charismatic Leadership, exploring the transformative impact it has on individuals, teams, and organizations.

1. **Visionary Outlook:**

   - Charismatic leaders possess not just a vision, but a compelling and aspirational vision of the future. This vision is ambitious yet realistic, inspiring others to reach for new heights.
   - They communicate this vision with clarity and passion, painting a vivid picture of what success looks like and how it will benefit the organization and its stakeholders.
   - Charismatic leaders continually reinforce the vision, keeping it at the forefront of everyone's minds and rallying support behind it, even in the face of challenges.

2. **Inspiring Communication:**

   - Charismatic leaders are adept at using language, tone, and body language to convey their message in a captivating and persuasive manner.

- They tell stories that resonate with their audience, appealing to emotions and values to inspire action.
- These leaders are also skilled listeners, actively engaging with their followers, understanding their concerns, and addressing them with empathy and understanding.

3. **Confidence and Self-Assurance:**

- Confidence is a hallmark trait of charismatic leaders. They exude self-assurance and conviction in their abilities and the vision they espouse.
- This confidence is infectious, inspiring confidence in others and reassuring them that they are on the right path.
- Charismatic leaders are unafraid to take risks and embrace uncertainty, demonstrating courage and resilience in the face of adversity.

4. **Empathy and Emotional Intelligence:**

- Despite their strong persona, charismatic leaders are deeply attuned to the emotions and needs of others.
- They demonstrate empathy by understanding the perspectives and experiences of their followers, fostering a sense of belonging and mutual respect.
- Emotional intelligence allows charismatic leaders to navigate complex interpersonal dynamics, build strong relationships, and inspire trust and loyalty.

5. **Authenticity and Integrity:**

- Authenticity is a core value for charismatic leaders. They remain true to themselves and their values, avoiding pretense or artifice.

- Their actions align with their words, and they lead by example, earning the trust and respect of their followers through their integrity and honesty.
- Charismatic leaders are transparent in their communication, admitting mistakes, and sharing both successes and failures openly.

6. **Charismatic Presence:**

- Charismatic leaders possess a magnetic presence that commands attention and inspires admiration.
- Their energy and enthusiasm are contagious, energizing and motivating others to action.
- Charismatic leaders cultivate a positive and uplifting atmosphere, creating a sense of excitement and possibility wherever they go.

7. **Transformational Impact:**

- Ultimately, charismatic leaders have a profound transformational impact on individuals, teams, and organizations.
- They inspire others to achieve their full potential, fostering innovation, creativity, and excellence.
- Charismatic leaders leave a lasting legacy, shaping the culture and direction of their organizations and inspiring future generations of leaders to follow in their footsteps.

In conclusion, Charismatic Leadership represents a powerful force for transformation, driving positive change and inspiring greatness in individuals, teams, and organizations. By embodying the fundamental principles of vision, communication, confidence, empathy, authenticity, presence, and impact, charismatic leaders leave an indelible mark on the world around them. They create cultures of innovation, collaboration, and excellence, fostering environments where individuals are empowered to unleash their full potential and contribute to shared goals. As we reflect on the impact of Charismatic Leadership, we are reminded of its enduring legacy and its ability to shape the course of history, leaving a profound and lasting imprint on the hearts and minds of all who are touched by its influence.

Theoretical Frameworks for Charismatic Leadership

Charismatic Leadership framework provides a unique perspective, emphasizing different aspects of this influential leadership style.

1. **Weber's Charismatic Leadership Theory:**

   - Max Weber, a sociologist, introduced the concept of charismatic leadership as one of the three types of authority (alongside traditional and legal-rational authority).
   - According to Weber, charismatic leaders derive their authority from followers' personal devotion and belief in the leader's exceptional qualities.
   - Charismatic authority is often revolutionary, challenging existing structures and introducing significant changes.

2. **Conger and Kanungo's Charismatic Leadership Model:**

   - Conger and Kanungo expanded on Weber's ideas, proposing a model that identifies specific behaviours associated with charismatic leaders.
   - They highlighted behaviours such as articulating an appealing vision, exhibiting confidence, expressing high expectations, and using powerful, emotive language.
   - The model emphasizes the leader's ability to inspire and influence followers through personal qualities and behaviours.

3. **House's Path Goal Theory:**

- Robert House's Path-Goal Theory incorporates elements of charismatic leadership by focusing on how leaders motivate followers to achieve goals.
- In this theory, leaders adopt different styles, including charismatic leadership, based on the characteristics of followers and the work environment.
- Charismatic leaders, according to this theory, clarify goals, provide a vision, and inspire subordinates to achieve exceptional performance.

4. **Shamir, House, and Arthur's Transformational Leadership Theory:**

- This theory builds on the concept of charismatic leadership but expands it into the broader framework of transformational leadership.
- Transformational leaders, including those with charismatic qualities, inspire and motivate followers by appealing to their higher-order needs and values.
- The theory emphasizes the leader's ability to elevate followers beyond self-interest, fostering a sense of collective purpose.

5. **Avolio and Yammarino Charismatic Leadership Theory:**

- Avolio and Yammarino proposed a model that incorporates both leader behaviors and attributes in understanding charismatic leadership.
- They identified specific behaviors, such as articulating a vision, providing high expectations, expressing confidence, and using symbolic actions, as central to charismatic leadership.

- The model also acknowledges the importance of followers' perceptions and attributions in charismatic leadership dynamics.

6. **Bass's Full Range Leadership Model:**

   - Bernard Bass extended the transformational leadership theory, incorporating charismatic leadership as one component of the full range of leadership behaviors.
   - In this model, charismatic leadership is part of the transformational leadership style, characterized by inspirational motivation, idealized influence, individualized consideration, and intellectual stimulation.

What motivates individuals to adopt a Charismatic approach to leadership?

The motivations for adopting charismatic leadership are diverse and often arise from a combination of personal attributes, values, and the belief in the transformative potential of charismatic leadership.

1. **Desire for Influence and Impact:**

   - Charismatic leaders are often driven by a deep-seated desire to make a significant impact on their followers and the organizations they lead.
   - The motivation stems from a belief in the transformative power of their vision and the ability to inspire positive change.

2. **Passion for a Compelling Vision:**

   - Charismatic leaders are often driven by a deep-seated desire to make a significant impact on their followers and the organizations they lead.

- The motivation stems from a belief in the transformative power of their vision and the ability to inspire positive change.

3. **Personal Conviction and Confidence:**

- Charismatic leaders possess a strong personal conviction in their abilities and the validity of their vision.
- Motivated by an unwavering self-confidence, they believe in their capacity to lead others towards shared goals and objectives.

4. **Recognition of Personal Charisma:**

- Individuals with charismatic qualities may be motivated to leverage their natural charm and appeal to lead effectively.
- The recognition of their personal charisma becomes a driving force, prompting them to adopt a leadership style that aligns with their innate qualities.

5. **Innate Leadership Aspirations:**

- Some individuals inherently aspire to leadership roles, and charismatic leadership offers a dynamic and influential approach to fulfilling these aspirations.
- The motivation lies in the desire to be at the forefront of guiding and inspiring others.

6. **Alignment with Transformational Goals:**

- Charismatic leaders often see their approach as aligned with transformational goals, where they aim to elevate followers and organizations to new levels of achievement.

- The motivation is rooted in the belief that charismatic leadership can bring about positive and transformative change.

7. **Response to Challenging Circumstances:**

   - In times of uncertainty or crisis, individuals may be motivated to adopt a charismatic leadership style as a response to challenging circumstances.
   - The belief that a charismatic approach can rally and inspire people during adversity becomes a compelling motivator.

8. **Desire for Personal Legacy:**

   - Charismatic leaders are often motivated by the desire to leave a lasting legacy.
   - The belief that their influence and impact can endure beyond their tenure drives them to adopt a charismatic leadership style.

9. **Recognition for Followers' Needs:**

   - Charismatic leaders may be motivated by a genuine recognition of followers' needs for inspiration, direction, and a sense of purpose.
   - The motivation to meet these needs through a charismatic leadership style stems from a genuine concern for the well-being and development of followers.

10. **Acknowledgement of Leadership Effectiveness:**

    - Charismatic leaders may be motivated by the acknowledgment that their charismatic approach is effective in achieving organizational goals and fostering a positive organizational culture.

Manifestation of Charismatic Leadership in Day-to-Day Leadership Practices

The philosophy of charismatic leadership is not just about grand gestures but manifests in the everyday actions and behaviors of leaders. It involves consistently embodying the qualities that inspire and motivate, creating a positive and dynamic work environment.

1. **Effective Communication:**

   Charismatic leaders excel in effective communication. They articulate a compelling vision with passion and clarity, using powerful language to inspire and motivate their followers.

   Manifestation: Regular communication sessions, town hall meetings, and one-on-one interactions to share the vision and reinforce organizational values.

2. **Building Trust and Rapport:**

   Charismatic leaders focus on building trust and rapport with their followers. They establish strong personal connections, making themselves approachable and relatable.

   Manifestation: Regular engagement, active listening, and demonstrating empathy to create a supportive and trusting environment.

3. **Setting High Expectations:**

   Charismatic leaders set high expectations for themselves and their followers. They believe in the potential of their team to achieve exceptional outcomes.

Manifestation: Clearly defining challenging goals, encouraging innovation, and expecting a commitment to excellence from each team member.

4. **Inspiring Confidence:**

Charismatic leaders exude self-confidence and inspire confidence in their followers. They remain calm and optimistic, even in the face of challenges.

Manifestation: Projecting confidence through body language, maintaining composure during crises, and expressing belief in the team's capabilities.

5. **Storytelling and Vision Casting:**

Charismatic leaders use storytelling to convey their vision and goals. They create a narrative that resonates with the values and aspirations of their followers.

Manifestation: Sharing anecdotes, illustrating successes, and using metaphorical language to make the vision relatable and inspiring.

6. **Active Engagement and Participation:**

Charismatic leaders actively engage with their teams, fostering a sense of involvement and participation. They are visible leaders who lead by example.

Manifestation: Participating in team activities, involving themselves in decision-making processes, and being hands-on in addressing challenges.

7. **Adaptability and Flexibility:**

Charismatic leaders demonstrate adaptability and flexibility in their leadership approach. They adjust their strategies based on changing circumstances.

Manifestation: Embracing change openly, encouraging innovation, and demonstrating flexibility in response to dynamic situations.

8. **Positive Reinforcement:**

Charismatic leaders use positive reinforcement to motivate their teams. They acknowledge and celebrate achievements, fostering a positive organizational culture.

Manifestation: Recognizing individual and team accomplishments, expressing appreciation, and providing constructive feedback.

9. **Charismatic Presence:**

Charismatic leaders have a charismatic presence that commands attention. They use their physical and vocal presence to influence and captivate.

Manifestation: Engaging public speaking, effective use of body language, and projecting a charismatic aura during team interactions.

10. **Empowerment and Delegation:**

Charismatic leaders empower their followers and delegate responsibilities. They trust their team members and encourage autonomy.

Manifestation: Delegating tasks based on individual strengths, providing opportunities for growth, and fostering a culture of empowerment.

Real Life Examples Illustrating Leaders who Exemplify Charismatic Leadership Framework

Below are a few real-life examples which illustrate how leaders with charismatic qualities can have a profound impact on diverse fields, ranging from civil rights and politics to technology and entertainment. Their ability to inspire, motivate, and articulate compelling visions showcases the influence of charismatic leadership on shaping positive outcomes.

1. **Martin Luther King Jr.:**

    - *Charismatic Leadership Style*: Martin Luther King Jr. was a charismatic leader during the American civil rights movement. His charisma lay in his powerful oratory, unwavering commitment to justice, and ability to inspire masses.

    - *Impact:* King's charismatic leadership played a pivotal role in mobilizing people for the cause of civil rights. His iconic "I Have a Dream" speech remains a powerful testament to his ability to captivate and inspire a nation.

2. **Steve Jobs:**

    - *Charismatic Leadership Style*: Steve Jobs, co-founder of Apple Inc., was known for his charismatic leadership. His ability to articulate a compelling vision for innovation, coupled with his dynamic presentation style, inspired both employees and consumers.

- *Impact:* Jobs' charismatic leadership contributed to the success of Apple, shaping it into one of the most innovative and influential technology companies. His product launches, marked by his charismatic presentations, became legendary in the business world.

3. **Oprah Winfrey:**

- *Charismatic Leadership Style:* Oprah Winfrey, a media mogul and talk show host, possesses a charismatic leadership style characterized by her authenticity, empathy, and ability to connect with audiences.
- *Impact:* Oprah's charisma has had a profound impact on her influence in the media and entertainment industry. Her ability to engage and relate to diverse audiences has made her a cultural icon and a positive force for change.

4. **Winston Churchill:**

- *Charismatic Leadership Style:* Winston Churchill, the British Prime Minister during World War II, exhibited charismatic leadership through his powerful speeches, resolve in the face of adversity, and ability to uplift the spirits of the British people.
- *Impact:* Churchill's charismatic leadership played a crucial role in rallying the nation during the war. His speeches, such as "We Shall Fight on the Beaches," are cited as examples of charismatic communication that inspired courage and determination.

5. **Nelson Mandela:**

- *Charismatic Leadership Style:* Nelson Mandela, the anti-apartheid revolutionary and former President of South

Africa, exhibited charismatic leadership through his vision of reconciliation, forgiveness, and unity.

- *Impact:* Mandela's charismatic leadership was instrumental in the transition to a democratic South Africa. His ability to unite a divided nation and inspire hope for a better future showcased the transformative impact of charismatic leadership.

6. **Elon Musk:**

- *Charismatic Leadership Style:* Elon Musk, the CEO of Tesla and SpaceX, displays charismatic leadership through his bold vision for the future of technology, space exploration, and sustainability.
- *Impact:* Musk's charismatic leadership has played a role in the success and innovation of his companies. His ability to convey a vision for transformative technologies has garnered widespread attention and support.

7. **Barack Obama:**

- *Charismatic Leadership Style:* Barack Obama, the 44th President of the United States, demonstrated charismatic leadership through his inspirational speeches, relatable demeanor, and message of hope and change.
- *Impact:* Obama's charismatic leadership was a key factor in his political rise and presidency. His ability to connect with diverse audiences and articulate a unifying vision contributed to his historic election and two terms in office.

Strategies for cultivating Charismatic Leadership framework

Cultivating Charismatic Leadership is a deliberate and ongoing process that requires individuals to proactively develop and refine specific traits, skills, and behaviors that embody the essence of this influential leadership style. It involves a deep commitment to personal growth and self-awareness, as well as a genuine desire to inspire and empower others. Here are some comprehensive strategies for cultivating Charismatic Leadership:

1. **Clarify Your Vision**:

   - Begin by taking time to deeply reflect on your personal and professional goals, as well as the overarching mission of your team or organization.
   - Articulate a clear and compelling vision that outlines the desired future state and inspires others to rally behind it.
   - Ensure that your vision is aspirational, yet realistic, and resonates with the values and aspirations of those you lead.
   - Communicate your vision consistently and passionately, using storytelling and vivid imagery to make it tangible and compelling for your team members.

2. **Develop Charismatic Communication Skills**:

   - Enhance your communication skills by practicing active listening, empathetic communication, and effective storytelling.
   - Pay attention to your nonverbal cues, such as body language and facial expressions, to convey confidence, warmth, and authenticity.
   - Tailor your message to your audience, using language and examples that resonate with their experiences and aspirations.
   - Practice delivering speeches, presentations, and messages with passion, energy, and conviction, leaving a lasting impact on your listeners.

3. **Build Confidence and Self-Assurance:**

- Cultivate a strong sense of self-confidence by recognizing your strengths, accomplishments, and unique qualities as a leader.

- Develop resilience in the face of setbacks and challenges, viewing them as opportunities for growth and learning.

- Take calculated risks and step outside your comfort zone, embracing uncertainty with courage and conviction.

- Seek feedback from trusted mentors and colleagues to validate your abilities and gain valuable insights for self-improvement.

4. **Enhance Empathy and Emotional Intelligence:**

- Practice empathy by actively listening to others, seeking to understand their perspectives, feelings, and needs.

- Cultivate emotional intelligence by recognizing and regulating your own emotions, as well as empathizing with the emotions of others.

- Foster a culture of psychological safety within your team or organization, where team members feel valued, respected, and understood.

- Use empathy as a tool for building trust, fostering collaboration, and strengthening relationships with your team members.

5. **Lead with Authenticity and Integrity:**

- Lead by example and demonstrate authenticity and integrity in all your actions and decisions.

- Be transparent and honest in your communication, sharing both successes and failures openly with your team members.

- Align your actions with your values and principles, and hold yourself accountable for maintaining ethical standards and moral conduct.
- Build trust and credibility with your team members by consistently demonstrating honesty, reliability, and fairness in your leadership.

6. **Cultivate a Charismatic Presence**:

- Develop a magnetic presence that commands attention and inspires admiration by projecting confidence, energy, and enthusiasm.
- Pay attention to your body language, posture, and vocal tone, ensuring that they convey warmth, positivity, and authenticity.
- Cultivate a positive and uplifting demeanor, radiating optimism and energy to those around you, even in challenging situations.
- Create a compelling personal brand that reflects your values, strengths, and leadership style, leaving a lasting impression on others.

7. **Inspire and Empower Others**:

- Empower and inspire your team members to achieve their full potential by providing them with opportunities for growth, learning, and development.
- Foster a culture of collaboration, innovation, and excellence within your team or organization, where everyone feels valued and motivated to contribute their best.
- Recognize and celebrate the achievements and contributions of your team members, providing them

with feedback, support, and encouragement along the way.

- Lead by example and serve as a role model for others, demonstrating the behaviors and attitudes that you wish to cultivate in your team members.

By implementing these strategies, leaders can cultivate Charismatic Leadership qualities and unlock their full potential to inspire and influence others. Remember that Charismatic Leadership is not about seeking personal glory, but rather about harnessing your influence to serve a higher purpose and inspire greatness in those around you.

Charismatic Leadership – My Observation and Experience

In my current role at Casagrand Builders, I had the opportunity to witness firsthand the transformative power of Charismatic Leadership through the actions of our MD & CEO, Mr. Arun. Mr. Arun possesses an innate ability to inspire and mobilize others toward a shared vision, leaving an indelible mark on the organization and its people.

One particular instance stands out vividly in my memory. Our company was facing a period of significant change and uncertainty due to market disruptions and internal challenges. Morale was low, and employees were feeling disheartened and demotivated.

Amidst this turbulence, Mr. Arun took center stage during a company-wide town hall meeting. With unwavering confidence and passion, he painted a compelling picture of the future—a future filled with innovation, growth, and opportunity. He spoke not just with words, but with genuine conviction and authenticity that resonated deeply with everyone in the room.

As he spoke, I observed the transformation taking place among the audience. Faces once filled with doubt and apprehension now lit up with hope and enthusiasm. Mr. Arun's charisma seemed to permeate the room, igniting a sense of purpose and excitement that was palpable.

But it wasn't just his words that inspired us; it was his actions. In the days and weeks following the town hall meeting, Mr. Arun led by example, rolling up his sleeves and working alongside employees at all levels of the organization. He listened attentively to their concerns, provided guidance and support, and celebrated their successes.

Under his charismatic leadership, a sense of unity and optimism began to take root within the organization. Teams collaborated more effectively, innovation flourished, and morale soared. Employees felt empowered to embrace change and pursue excellence, knowing that they had a visionary leader guiding them every step of the way.

Through Mr. Arun's example, I learned that Charismatic Leadership is not just about charisma or charm; it's about authenticity, passion, and a genuine commitment to a shared vision. It's about inspiring others to believe in themselves and their ability to achieve greatness, even in the face of adversity.

Mr. Arun's leadership has left a lasting impression on me, serving as a reminder of the profound impact that a charismatic leader can have on an organization and its people. His legacy continues to inspire me to strive for excellence and lead with passion, purpose, and authenticity in everything I do.

Conclusion

In the intricate tapestry of leadership, the thread of charisma weaves a compelling narrative of influence, inspiration, and impact. Charismatic Leadership, as explored in this chapter, stands as a beacon of extraordinary influence, where leaders possess the magnetic qualities that captivate hearts and minds. The journey through the characteristics and impact of charismatic leadership reveals not just a leadership style but a transformative force that shapes organizations, movements, and nations.

Charismatic leaders, as witnessed in the real-life examples, possess a unique ability to transcend conventional boundaries. Their exceptional communication skills, unwavering confidence, and the aura of influence create a resonance that galvanizes followers toward shared aspirations. Whether in the realm of civil rights, technology, or global politics, charismatic leaders leave an indelible mark on the collective consciousness, steering the course of history.

As we conclude this exploration of Charismatic Leadership, it is evident that charisma is not merely a trait but a dynamic force that can be cultivated and harnessed. Leaders who understand the art of inspiration, who can articulate a compelling vision, and who foster genuine connections can unlock the transformative potential of charisma. The impact of charismatic leadership extends beyond the individual leader, influencing organizational cultures, driving innovation, and shaping a legacy that endures.

Practical Exercises and Reflection Questions

These exercises and reflection questions are designed to encourage readers to actively apply and critically reflect on the concepts discussed in this chapter. They aim to bridge the gap between theory and practical application, fostering a deeper understanding of how leadership frameworks can be valuable tools in real-world leadership scenarios.

Practical Exercises

1. **Craft Your Visionary Message:**

    Exercise: Develop a short and impactful message that articulates your vision as a leader. Focus on clarity, passion, and inspiration.

    Reflection: How does your crafted message resonate with the key characteristics of charismatic leadership? How might it inspire others to align with your vision?

2. **Power your Presence:**

    Exercise: Practice projecting confidence and a charismatic presence in front of a mirror or with a trusted colleague. Pay attention to body language, tone, and facial expressions.

    Reflection: What adjustments can you make to enhance your physical and vocal presence? How might this influence your leadership interactions?

3. **Storytelling Mastery:**

    Exercise: Share a personal or professional anecdote in a way that captivates your audience. Emphasize emotions, vivid imagery, and a clear message.

Reflection: How did storytelling enhance your communication? In what situations can you leverage storytelling to convey your vision?

4. **Building Rapport:**

Exercise: Engage in one-on-one conversations with team members to build personal connections. Practice active listening and show genuine interest.

Reflection: What insights did you gain about your team members during these conversations? How can you use this knowledge to strengthen relationships?

Reflection Questions

1. **Identifying Charismatic Moments:**

When have you experienced moments of charismatic leadership, either as a leader or a follower? What specific behaviors or qualities stood out in those instances?

2. **Personal Charismatic Attributes:**

Reflect on your own charismatic attributes. What qualities do you believe contribute to your charisma? In what ways can you further develop these attributes?

3. **Inspiring through Communication:**

Think about a challenging situation where you need to inspire and motivate your team. How can you apply charismatic communication techniques to address and navigate this challenge?

4. **Adapting Charismatic Leadership:**

Consider different leadership scenarios (e.g., crisis, innovation, team building). How might you adapt your charismatic leadership style to effectively respond to each situation?

5. **Feedback and Improvement:**

Seek feedback from colleagues or team members on your leadership style. What aspects of charismatic leadership do they perceive in your interactions? How can you improve in this regard?

6. **Applying Charismatic Leadership in Teams:**

Reflect on your team dynamics. How might charismatic leadership principles be applied to enhance collaboration, innovation, and a positive team culture?

Chapter 12

Leader-Member Exchange (LMX) Theory

In the dynamic landscape of leadership theory, the Leader-Member Exchange (LMX) Theory stands as a cornerstone for understanding the intricate dynamics between leaders and their followers. This chapter delves into the foundational principles of LMX Theory, exploring how the quality of leader-member relationships can shape organizational outcomes and individual performance.

As we embark on this exploration, it's essential to recognize the pivotal role that interpersonal relationships play in leadership effectiveness. LMX Theory offers invaluable insights into how leaders form unique exchanges with their followers, leading to varying degrees of trust, support, and collaboration.

Throughout this chapter, we will uncover the underlying mechanisms of LMX Theory, examining how leaders establish differentiated relationships with their team members based on mutual respect, trust, and reciprocity. We will explore the implications of high-quality LMX relationships, such as enhanced job satisfaction, increased organizational commitment, and improved performance outcomes.

Moreover, we will investigate practical strategies for fostering positive leader-member exchanges within organizations, empowering leaders to cultivate strong, supportive relationships with their team members. By understanding the nuances of LMX Theory and its implications for leadership practice, readers will gain valuable insights into building effective leader-member relationships and driving organizational success.

Join us as we unravel the intricacies of Leader-Member Exchange Theory and discover how fostering positive relationships between leaders and followers can unlock the full potential of individuals and teams within organizations.

Definition and Key Concepts

Leader-Member Exchange (LMX) Theory, also known as Vertical Dyad Linkage Theory, is a leadership framework that shifts the focus from a one-size-fits-all approach to recognizing the individualized relationships between leaders and their followers. LMX Theory asserts that leaders form distinct, unique relationships with each of their subordinates, shaping the nature of their interactions and influence.

Key Concepts

- **Vertical Dyad:**

  LMX Theory emphasizes the importance of leader-subordinate dyads, recognizing that each dyad is unique. It challenges the traditional view of leader-follower relationships as uniform and explores the dynamic exchanges that occur within these dyads.

- **Reciprocity:**

  LMX Theory is built on the principle of reciprocity. As leaders invest time and resources in building high-quality relationships with their subordinates, they expect a return on that investment in terms of commitment, trust, and performance.

- **In-Group and Out-Group:**

  LMX Theory introduces the concepts of in-group and out-group. In-group members enjoy a closer, more personalized relationship with the leader, characterized by higher levels of trust, shared goals, and collaboration. Out-group members, on the other hand, have a more transactional and formal relationship.

The Continuum of Leader-Member Relationships

LMX Theory posits that leader-member relationships exist on a continuum, ranging from high-quality, personalized exchanges to more transactional, formal exchanges. Understanding this continuum is crucial for grasping the diversity of relationships within an organization.

Continuum Highlights

- **High – Quality Exchanges (In-Group):**

  Leaders engage in high-quality exchanges with certain subordinates, forming the in-group. These relationships are characterized by mutual respect, trust, and a sense of partnership. In-group members often receive more attention, resources, and opportunities for growth.

- **Low – Quality Exchanges (Out-Group):**

  Out-group members experience lower-quality exchanges, marked by more formal, transactional interactions. These relationships lack the depth and personalization seen in in-group exchanges.

- **Dynamic Nature:**

  The leader-member relationship is not static; it evolves over time. Subordinates can transition between in-group and out-group status based on their performance, commitment, and the leader's perception.

The role of Trust and Collaboration

- **Trust:**

  Trust is a cornerstone of LMX Theory. In high-quality exchanges, there is a foundation of trust between the leader and the in-group members. This trust facilitates open communication, risk-taking, and a sense of psychological safety.

- **Collaboration:**

  Collaboration is more pronounced within the in-group, where leaders and members work together toward shared goals. In-group members feel a sense of ownership and commitment to the leader's vision, fostering a collaborative environment.

Understanding the foundational principles of LMX Theory provides leaders with a nuanced perspective on their relationships with subordinates. By acknowledging the individualized nature of these exchanges and recognizing the role of trust and collaboration, leaders can navigate the continuum of leader-member relationships to enhance organizational effectiveness and team dynamics.

In-Group and Out-Group Dynamics

Characteristics of In-Group Relationships

In-Group relationships within the Leader-Member Exchange (LMX) Theory represent high-quality exchanges between leaders and specific subordinates. These relationships are characterized by unique dynamics that set them apart from more formal, transactional interactions. Understanding the characteristics of in-group relationships is essential for comprehending how leaders and followers collaborate within these close-knit units.

Key Characteristics

1. **Trust and Mutual Respect:**

   In-Group relationships are built on a foundation of trust and mutual respect. Leaders and in-group members share a level of familiarity that fosters a sense of trust, enabling open communication and collaboration.

2. **Shared Goals and Vision:**

   In-Group members align with the leader's vision and organizational goals. There is a shared sense of purpose, and in-group members are often more deeply involved in decision-making processes.

3. **Greater Attention and Resources:**

   Leaders invest more time and resources in nurturing in-group relationships. In-Group members may receive additional support, mentoring, and opportunities for professional development.

4. **Psychological Safety:**

   In-Group members feel psychologically safe within the relationship, allowing for honest feedback, innovation, and a willingness to take calculated risks.

Implications of Out-Group Dynamics

Out-Group dynamics in LMX Theory represent relationships that are more formal, transactional, and lack the depth seen in in-group exchanges. Examining the implications of out-group dynamics provides insights into how these relationships impact both individuals and the organization as a whole.

Key Implications

1. **Limited Access to Resources:**

   Out-Group members may have limited access to the leader's time, attention, and resources. This can impact their professional growth and development within the organization.

2. **Transactional Interactions:**

   Interactions within out-group dynamics are often transactional, focusing on task-related discussions rather than fostering a deeper, more personal connection.

3. **Lower Levels of Trust:**

   Trust levels are typically lower in out-group dynamics. The lack of familiarity and personalization may lead to a more formal and guarded communication style.

4. **Reduced Involvement in Decision-Making:**

   Out-Group members may have limited involvement in organizational decision-making processes, contributing to a sense of detachment from the overarching goals and vision.

Communication Patterns within In-Group and Out-Group Contexts

Communication plays a pivotal role in leader-member exchanges. Examining the communication patterns within in-group and out-group contexts sheds light on how information flows and relationships are maintained.

Communication Patterns

1. **Open and Transparent Communication (In-Group):**

   In-Group relationships foster open and transparent communication. Leaders and in-group members feel comfortable sharing ideas, concerns, and feedback.

2. **Task-Oriented Communication (Out-Group):**

   Communication within out-group dynamics tends to be more task-oriented, focusing on the completion of assigned responsibilities rather than building interpersonal connections.

3. **Collaborative Decision-Making (In-Group):**

   In-Group members often participate in collaborative decision-making processes, contributing to a sense of ownership and commitment.

Understanding these dynamics provides leaders with insights into how the quality of leader-member exchanges influences team dynamics, organizational culture, and overall effectiveness. Recognizing the characteristics and implications of in-group and out-group dynamics enables leaders to navigate these relationships strategically, fostering a positive and inclusive workplace environment.

Theoretical Frameworks for LMX Leadership framework

Leader-Member Exchange (LMX) theory is a leadership framework rooted in the study of leader-subordinate relationships. The theoretical underpinnings of LMX encompass several key concepts:

1. **Social Exchange Theory:**

   - *Explanation*: LMX draws heavily from social exchange theory, which posits that social interactions are based on the principle of reciprocity. In the context of LMX, leaders and followers engage in a social exchange where they contribute to and receive benefits from the relationship.

- *Application to LMX*: LMX suggests that leaders and followers form unique exchange relationships characterized by mutual obligations and benefits. These relationships are built on a foundation of reciprocity, trust, and the expectation of fair treatment.

2. **Role-Making Theory:**

   - *Explanation*: Role-making theory proposes that individuals actively shape their roles within organizations. In the context of LMX, both leaders and followers play an active role in defining the nature of their relationship and the expectations associated with it.
   - *Application to LMX*: LMX emphasizes the dynamic and evolving nature of leader-subordinate relationships. Individuals have the agency to shape the quality and content of their exchanges, contributing to the unique nature of each LMX relationship.

3. **Social Identity Theory:**

   - *Explanation*: Social identity theory suggests that individuals categorize themselves and others into social groups, and their self-concept is tied to these group memberships. In LMX, social identity plays a role in how individuals perceive their roles within the in-group or out-group.
   - *Application to LMX*: LMX introduces the concepts of in-group and out-group dynamics, where individuals

within the in-group have higher-quality relationships with the leader. Social identity influences the formation of these groups and the associated dynamics.

4. **Trait-Based Theories:**

- *Explanation*: Trait-based theories of leadership focus on identifying specific traits and characteristics that distinguish effective leaders. In the context of LMX, certain leader and follower traits may influence the formation and quality of exchange relationships.

- *Application to LMX*: LMX recognizes that individual differences, including personality traits and characteristics, can impact the leader-follower relationship. Traits such as openness, agreeableness, and conscientiousness may contribute to the quality of LMX relationships.

5. **Norms of Reciprocity:**

- *Explanation*: Norms of reciprocity refer to the social expectation that individuals will respond to positive actions with positive actions and vice versa. In LMX, reciprocity is a fundamental aspect of the exchange relationship between leaders and followers.

- *Application to LMX*: LMX relationships are guided by norms of reciprocity, where both leaders and followers are expected to contribute positively to the relationship. The mutual exchange of support, trust, and cooperation is essential for the maintenance of a high-quality LMX relationship.

These theoretical frameworks collectively contribute to the understanding of Leader-Member Exchange, shedding light on the social, psychological, and relational dynamics that characterize effective leadership exchanges within organizations.

What motivates individuals to adopt a LMX approach to leadership?

Individuals may be motivated to adopt a Leader-Member Exchange (LMX) approach to leadership for several reasons, driven by both personal and organizational considerations. Here are key motivations:

1. **Increased Opportunities for Growth:**

   - *Motivation:* Individuals may be motivated by the potential for professional growth and development. In a high-quality leader-member exchange, leaders provide guidance, mentorship, and opportunities for skill development.

   - *Impact:* A focus on growth opportunities enhances individuals' skills and capabilities, making them more valuable contributors to the organization. This can lead to career advancement and increased job satisfaction.

2. **Enhanced Job Satisfaction:**

   - *Motivation*: Individuals are motivated by the prospect of increased job satisfaction through positive leader-member relationships. LMX fosters a supportive work environment, where team members feel valued and understood.

   - *Impact:* Higher job satisfaction can lead to increased employee morale, engagement, and a positive attitude toward work. This, in turn, contributes to higher productivity and retention.

3. **Sense of Belonging and Inclusion:**

- *Motivation:* Individuals seek a sense of belonging and inclusion within the workplace. LMX emphasizes personalized relationships, creating a feeling of being part of an in-group.

- *Impact:* When individuals feel a sense of belonging, they are more likely to contribute positively to team dynamics. This sense of inclusion can lead to increased collaboration, effective communication, and a stronger team culture.

4. **Positive Work Relationships:**

- *Motivation*: Individuals are motivated by the desire for positive relationships with their leaders. LMX focuses on building strong interpersonal connections, fostering trust and open communication.

- *Impact:* Positive work relationships contribute to a healthy work environment, reducing conflicts and enhancing team cohesion. Individuals are more likely to be engaged and committed when they experience positive interactions with their leaders.

5. **Alignment with Organizational Values:**

- *Motivation:* Individuals may be motivated by the alignment of LMX principles with organizational values. LMX emphasizes fairness, inclusivity, and collaboration, which resonates with employees who value these principles.

- *Impact*: When leadership practices align with organizational values, individuals are more likely to feel connected to the broader mission and goals. This alignment enhances organizational culture and contributes to a positive workplace.

6. **Increased Job Performance Recognition:**

   - *Motivation*: Individuals seek recognition and acknowledgment for their contributions. LMX encourages leaders to recognize and reward the efforts of team members.

   - *Impact:* Recognizing individual contributions positively impacts morale and job satisfaction. It motivates individuals to consistently perform at their best, knowing that their efforts are valued and acknowledged.

7. **Higher Organizational Commitment:**

   - *Motivation*: Individuals may be motivated by the potential for higher organizational commitment. LMX emphasizes building strong bonds between leaders and team members, fostering a sense of loyalty.

   - *Impact:* Higher organizational commitment leads to increased employee retention and a willingness to go above and beyond in support of organizational goals. This commitment contributes to overall organizational success.

Understanding and recognizing these motivations can guide leaders in implementing and sustaining LMX principles within their leadership approach. By addressing these motivations, leaders can foster a positive work environment and build strong, productive relationships with their team members.

Manifestation of LMX Leadership framework in Day-to-Day Leadership Practices

The manifestation of Leader-Member Exchange (LMX) leadership framework in day-to-day leadership practices involves specific behaviors and interactions between leaders and team members. Here's how LMX principles can be reflected in everyday leadership practices:

1. **Individualized Interactions:**

   Manifestation: Leaders practicing LMX engage in individualized interactions with each team member. They take time to understand the unique strengths, needs, and preferences of everyone.

   Examples:

   - Personalized feedback sessions tailored to each team member's development goals.
   - Regular one-on-one meetings to discuss career aspirations and challenges.

2. **Open Communication Channels:**

   Manifestation: LMX leaders prioritize open communication channels, creating an environment where team members feel comfortable expressing their thoughts and concerns.

   Examples:

   - Regular team meetings where all members are encouraged to share ideas and opinions.
   - Accessibility of leaders for informal discussions and feedback.

3. **Collaborative Decision-Making:**

Manifestation: LMX leaders involve team members in the decision-making process, recognizing their expertise and perspectives.

Examples:

- Seeking input from team members when making project-related decisions.
- Involving the team in setting goals and objectives for the group.

4. **Support for Professional Growth:**

Manifestation: LMX leaders actively support the professional growth of their team members, providing opportunities for skill development and advancement.

Examples:

- Offering mentorship and guidance on career development paths.
- Providing access to training programs and workshops.

5. **Recognition of Individual Contributions:**

Manifestation: LMX leaders acknowledge and recognize the individual contributions of team members, expressing gratitude for their efforts.

Examples:

- Publicly acknowledging accomplishments during team meetings.
- Providing personalized recognition, such as shout-outs or awards.

6. **Fair and Equitable Treatment:**

Manifestation: LMX leaders demonstrate fairness and equitable treatment, ensuring that all team members feel valued and included.

Examples:

- Assigning tasks and responsibilities based on individual strengths and interests.
- Addressing conflicts promptly and impartially.

7. **Building Trust and Rapport:**

Manifestation: LMX leaders focus on building trust and rapport with each team member, creating a positive and supportive relationship.

Examples:

- Investing time in team-building activities to strengthen interpersonal connections.
- Demonstrating consistency and reliability in leadership actions.

8. **Flexibility and Adaptability:**

Manifestation: LMX leaders exhibit flexibility and adaptability in their leadership approach, adjusting to the evolving needs and preferences of team members.

Examples:

- Being open to alternative work arrangements that suit individual preferences.
- Modifying leadership strategies based on changing project requirements.

9. **Promotion of Inclusivity:**

Manifestation: LMX leaders promote inclusivity by ensuring that all team members, regardless of their position, have opportunities to contribute and be heard.

Examples:

- Encouraging introverted team members to share their perspectives.
- Implementing inclusive practices in decision-making to avoid favoritism.

10. **Empowerment of Team Members:**

Manifestation: LMX leaders empower team members by delegating responsibilities and entrusting them with meaningful tasks

Examples:

- Allowing team members to take the lead on specific projects.
- Providing autonomy and decision-making authority within defined boundaries.

By consistently integrating these practices into their daily leadership approach, LMX leaders cultivate strong, positive, and mutually beneficial relationships with their team members. This, in turn, contributes to a healthy organizational culture and enhances overall team performance and satisfaction.

Real Life Examples Illustrating Leaders who Exemplify Charismatic Leadership Framework

Real-life examples of leaders who exemplify the Leader-Member Exchange (LMX) leadership framework showcase the application of

LMX principles in various organizational contexts. Here are a few examples:

1. **Indra Nooyi (Former CEO of PepsiCo):**

   - *LMX Exemplification:*

     - ✓ Indra Nooyi, during her tenure as the CEO of PepsiCo, was known for building strong, personalized relationships with her top executives.
     - ✓ She emphasized open communication and collaboration, fostering a culture where leaders felt comfortable sharing their opinions and ideas.

   - *Impact:*

     - ✓ PepsiCo's performance and innovation were attributed, in part, to the collaborative relationships between Nooyi and her leadership team.
     - ✓ The emphasis on individualized exchanges contributed to a more engaged and motivated top leadership group.

2. **Satya Nadella (CEO of Microsoft):**

   - *LMX Exemplification:*

     - ✓ Satya Nadella has demonstrated a leadership style that involves close collaboration with his top executives and key team members.
     - ✓ He encourages a culture of openness and inclusivity, valuing diverse perspectives within the leadership team.

- *Impact:*

  - ✓ Microsoft's successful transition to a cloud-first strategy and increased focus on innovation is credited, in part, to Nadella's inclusive leadership style.
  - ✓ The emphasis on individualized exchanges has contributed to a positive organizational culture and improved employee engagement.

3. **Mary Dillon (Former CEO of Ulta Beauty):**

- *LMX Exemplification:*

  - ✓ Mary Dillon was recognized for her emphasis on building strong relationships with her leadership team and employees at Ulta Beauty.
  - ✓ She prioritized regular communication and collaboration, creating an environment where team members felt valued.

- *Impact:*

  - ✓ Ulta Beauty's success in the highly competitive beauty and retail industry is attributed to Dillon's collaborative leadership style.
  - ✓ The focus on individualized exchanges has contributed to a positive workplace culture and employee satisfaction.

4. **Jeff Bezos (Founder and Former CEO of Amazon):**

- *LMX Exemplification:*

  - ✓ Jeff Bezos, known for his hands-on approach, has demonstrated a personalized leadership style with key executives at Amazon.

✓ He values direct and candid communication, creating a culture of shared responsibility and accountability.

- *Impact*:

  ✓ Amazon's rapid growth and innovation are, in part, attributed to Bezos's emphasis on individualized exchanges with key leaders.
  ✓ The focus on strong relationships has contributed to Amazon's ability to adapt to changing market dynamics.

These examples highlight how leaders who practice the principles of Leader-Member Exchange (LMX) foster strong relationships with their teams, leading to positive organizational outcomes. The emphasis on individualized exchanges, open communication, and collaboration contributes to a culture of trust, engagement, and innovation within these organizations.

Strategies for cultivating Leader-Member Exchange framework approach in leadership

Cultivating Leader-Member Exchange (LMX) Theory framework involves intentional efforts to foster positive relationships between leaders and their followers. Here are some strategies for cultivating LMX Theory framework:

Certainly! Let's delve deeper into each of the strategies for cultivating Leader-Member Exchange (LMX) Theory framework:

1. **Build Rapport and Trust:**

   - Invest time in building authentic relationships with your team members. Take a genuine interest in their lives, interests, and aspirations, and demonstrate empathy and understanding.

- Be approachable and accessible to your team members and encourage open communication and feedback. Create a supportive and non-judgmental environment where team members feel comfortable sharing their thoughts and concerns.

- Follow through on commitments and promises, and act with integrity and consistency in your interactions with your team. Trust is built through reliability, honesty, and transparency.

2. **Promote Two-Way Communication:**

   - Establish regular channels for communication, such as team meetings, one-on-one discussions, and virtual platforms, to facilitate ongoing dialogue between leaders and followers.

   - Encourage active listening by giving your full attention to your team members and acknowledging their perspectives and contributions. Practice empathy and seek to understand their viewpoints before offering your own.

   - Solicit feedback from your team members on a regular basis, and use this feedback to inform your leadership approach and decision-making. Demonstrate responsiveness to their input and show that their opinions are valued and respected.

3. **Offer Support and Development:**

   - Provide mentorship, coaching, and guidance to help your team members develop their skills and achieve their career goals. Offer constructive feedback and praise for their accomplishments, and provide opportunities for them to stretch and grow.

- Advocate for resources and support for your team members, whether it's additional training, professional development opportunities, or access to tools and technology that can enhance their performance.

- Be proactive in addressing any barriers or challenges that may impede your team members' progress, and offer your assistance and support in overcoming them.

4. **Clarify Expectations and Roles**:

- Set clear expectations for your team members regarding their roles, responsibilities, and performance standards. Provide clear direction and guidance on priorities, deadlines, and objectives, and ensure that everyone is aligned with the team's goals.

- Foster a sense of ownership and accountability among your team members by empowering them to make decisions and take initiative within their roles. Encourage autonomy and independence while providing support and guidance as needed.

- Regularly revisit and reassess roles and responsibilities to ensure that they align with the evolving needs of the team and the organization. Be open to adjusting expectations and roles as circumstances change.

5. **Empower Decision-Making**:

- Delegate authority and decision-making responsibilities to your team members, allowing them to take ownership of their work and contribute to the team's success.

Encourage them to think critically and creatively and empower them to make decisions independently within their areas of expertise.

- Provide guidance and support as needed, but avoid micromanaging or dictating every aspect of their work. Trust your team members to make sound decisions and respect their autonomy and judgment.

- Celebrate and recognize team members' contributions and successes, and encourage a culture of experimentation and learning from both successes and failures. Encourage risk-taking and innovation, and create a safe space for team members to explore new ideas and approaches.

6. **Manage Conflict Effectively:**

- Address conflicts and disagreements promptly and constructively, focusing on finding mutually beneficial solutions and preserving positive relationships. Encourage open dialogue and communication, and create opportunities for all parties to share their perspectives and concerns.

- Practice active listening and empathy when resolving conflicts, and seek to understand the underlying causes and motivations behind different viewpoints. Avoid making assumptions or assigning blame, and focus on finding common ground and moving forward together.

- Use conflict resolution techniques such as mediation, negotiation, and compromise to reach mutually acceptable outcomes. Encourage forgiveness and reconciliation, and promote a culture of understanding and respect among team members.

7. **Promote Inclusivity and Diversity:**

- Foster an inclusive and diverse work environment where all team members feel valued, respected, and included. Embrace diversity of thought, background, and perspective, and create opportunities for everyone to contribute their unique talents and insights.

- Ensure that all team members have equal access to resources, opportunities, and support, regardless of their background or identity. Champion diversity and inclusion initiatives within the organization, and advocate for policies and practices that promote fairness and equity.

- Create a culture of belonging where team members feel comfortable expressing themselves authentically and bringing their whole selves to work. Celebrate the richness of diversity and encourage collaboration and cooperation across different groups and identities.

8. **Lead by Example:**

- Model the behaviors and attitudes that you expect from your team members. Demonstrate integrity, honesty, and transparency in your actions and decisions, and hold yourself accountable to the same standards that you set for others.

- Show vulnerability and humility by admitting mistakes and seeking feedback from your team members. Lead with authenticity and authenticity, and strive to build genuine connections with your team members based on trust and respect.

- Be a role model for ethical leadership and responsible decision-making and inspire your team members to uphold these values in their own interactions and relationships. Lead by example and demonstrate your commitment to cultivating positive leader-member exchanges within your team.

By implementing these strategies, leaders can create a culture of trust, collaboration, and mutual respect within their teams, fostering positive leader-member exchanges and driving organizational success.

Leader-Member Exchange – My Observation and Experience

In a bustling corporate environment, I had the privilege of witnessing firsthand the application of Leader-Member Exchange (LMX) Theory in action. The story I'm about to share revolves around a seasoned executive, Lata, and her team of dedicated professionals in the marketing department with whom I used to interact with at Sterling Holidays.

Lata, the head of marketing, had a unique leadership style that emphasized building strong relationships with each member of her team. As a third-party observer, I noticed how Lata approached her interactions with her team members with genuine care and attention, embodying the principles of LMX Theory.

One particular incident stands out vividly in my memory. It was during a crucial project deadline when the team encountered unexpected challenges that threatened to derail the entire initiative. Instead of resorting to micromanagement or dictating solutions, Lata rallied her team together in a series of one-on-one meetings.

During these meetings, Lata took the time to listen attentively to each team member's perspective, concerns, and proposed solutions. She provided unwavering support and encouragement, acknowledging the unique strengths and capabilities of each individual. Lata fostered an environment of open communication and trust, where team members felt empowered to share their ideas and collaborate on finding creative solutions to overcome the obstacles.

Through Lata's leadership, the team developed a shared sense of ownership and accountability for the project's success. Each team member felt valued and appreciated, knowing that their contributions were integral to achieving the collective goals. Lata's approach exemplified the principles of LMX Theory, where high-quality leader-member exchanges are characterized by mutual respect, trust, and support.

As a result of Lata's leadership, the team not only met the project deadline but also exceeded expectations, delivering innovative solutions that garnered praise from senior management. The positive leader-member exchanges cultivated under Lata's guidance fostered a culture of collaboration and excellence within the marketing department, setting a precedent for future projects and initiatives.

This story serves as a testament to the transformative power of Leader-Member Exchange (LMX) Theory in driving organizational success. By prioritizing strong relationships and effective communication, leaders like Lata can unleash the full potential of their teams and create environments where individuals thrive and organizations flourish.

Conclusion

In the intricate landscape of leadership theories, the Leader-Member Exchange (LMX) framework emerges as a compelling and human-centric approach. As we conclude our exploration of LMX, we reflect on the fundamental principles that underpin its philosophy—personalized relationships, open communication, and collaboration.

LMX challenges the traditional top-down model, offering a paradigm where leaders and team members engage in a reciprocal dance of trust, respect, and shared goals. The real-life examples of leaders who have embraced LMX principles underscore its efficacy in diverse organizational settings.

As we traverse the chapters of this book, it becomes evident that LMX is not a mere theoretical concept but a dynamic force that transforms workplaces. The stories of leaders like Indra Nooyi, Satya Nadella, Mary Dillon, and Jeff Bezos showcase how investing in personalized exchanges creates a ripple effect, positively impacting organizational culture, employee satisfaction, and overall performance.

In our journey through LMX, we've witnessed its manifestation in day-to-day leadership practices—individualized interactions, open communication channels, collaborative decision-making, and an unwavering commitment to the growth of each team member. These practices not only define LMX leadership but also set the stage for thriving, innovative, and resilient organizations.

As we conclude this chapter, let us carry the essence of LMX into our own leadership journeys. Let us embrace the idea that leadership is not just a position but a relationship—a dynamic exchange that shapes the destiny of individuals and organizations alike. Through personalized interactions and shared visions, we can foster environments where everyone is empowered to contribute their best.

Practical Exercises and Reflection Questions

These exercises and reflection questions are designed to encourage readers to actively apply and critically reflect on the concepts discussed in this chapter. They aim to bridge the gap between theory and practical application, fostering a deeper understanding of how leadership frameworks can be valuable tools in real-world leadership scenarios.

Practical Exercises

1. **Reflect on Relationship Quality:**

   Exercise: Assess your current relationships within your team or organization. Identify one or two key relationships and evaluate the quality of the exchanges. Consider factors such as trust, communication, and mutual support.

   Reflection Questions:

   - What aspects contribute to the quality of these relationships?
   - Are there opportunities for improvement in how you exchange with these individuals?

2. **In-Group and Out-Group Analysis:**

   Exercise: Identify the in-group and out-group dynamics within your team or organization. Reflect on whether certain individuals receive preferential treatment or have higher-quality relationships with leaders.

   Reflection Questions:

   - How do in-group dynamics impact team dynamics and collaboration?

- What steps can be taken to promote inclusivity and minimize out-group dynamics?

3. **360 – Degree Feedback:**

Exercise: Seek feedback from colleagues, subordinates, and superiors regarding your leadership style and the quality of your exchanges. Use a 360-degree feedback tool to gather diverse perspectives.

Reflection Questions:

- What patterns or themes emerge from the feedback?
- In what ways can you enhance the quality of your leader-member exchanges based on this feedback?

4. **Role-Making Simulation:**

Exercise: Engage in a role-making simulation where you actively shape your role and responsibilities within the team. Discuss and negotiate with team members to establish clear expectations and contributions.

Reflection Questions:

- How did the negotiation process influence your role within the team?
- What insights did you gain about the importance of role-making in leader-member exchanges?

Reflection Questions for Individuals

1. **Self-Reflection on Reciprocity**

- How do I contribute to positive exchanges within my team or with my leader?

- In what ways can I enhance the reciprocity in my leader-member exchanges?

2. **Influence of Social Identity:**

   - How does my social identity impact my perception of in-group and out-group dynamics?
   - Are there biases or preferences that may be influencing my relationships?

3. **Traits and Relationship Quality:**

   - How do my personal traits and characteristics align with the traits associated with high-quality leader-member exchanges?
   - In what ways can I leverage my strengths to enhance relationship quality?

4. **Strategies for Enhancing LMX:**

   - What specific actions can I take to improve the quality of my leader-member exchanges?
   - How can I promote a culture of inclusivity and collaboration within my team?

These exercises and reflection questions aim to engage readers actively in assessing their own leader-member exchanges, promoting self-awareness, and encouraging intentional efforts to apply LMX principles in their unique leadership contexts.

Chapter 13

Distributive Leadership

In the ever-evolving landscape of leadership theory, Distributive Leadership emerges as a dynamic framework that challenges traditional notions of hierarchical leadership. Unlike conventional top-down approaches, Distributive Leadership recognizes leadership as a collective endeavor, distributed among various individuals within an organization. In this chapter, we explore the principles and practices of Distributive Leadership, delving into its significance in fostering innovation, collaboration, and empowerment within teams and organizations.

As we embark on this exploration, it's essential to understand the context in which Distributive Leadership operates. In today's fast-paced and complex business environment, organizations face increasingly multifaceted challenges that demand agility, adaptability, and creativity. Traditional leadership models, characterized by centralized decision-making and rigid hierarchies, often struggle to meet these demands effectively.

Distributive Leadership offers a compelling alternative, emphasizing the shared responsibility and collaborative efforts of multiple leaders across all levels of an organization. Rather than relying on a single figurehead at the helm, Distributive Leadership encourages the cultivation of leadership capabilities among all team members, enabling them to take ownership of their roles and contribute meaningfully to the organization's mission and goals.

Throughout this chapter, we will explore the principles that underpin Distributive Leadership, examine its practical applications in real-world contexts, and discuss strategies for implementing and fostering a Distributive Leadership culture within organizations. By embracing the principles of shared leadership and collective responsibility, organizations can unlock the full potential of their teams and adapt more effectively to the ever-changing demands of the modern business landscape. Join us as we delve into the transformative power of Distributive Leadership and its implications for the future of leadership practice.

Fundamental Principles of Distributive Leadership

Distributive Leadership is a contemporary leadership approach that challenges traditional hierarchical structures by distributing leadership responsibilities and decision-making authority across various individuals within an organization. Unlike the conventional top-down leadership models where power and influence are concentrated in the hands of a select few, Distributive Leadership recognizes that leadership can emerge from all levels and functions of an organization.

The fundamental principles of the Distributive Leadership framework encompass:

1. **Shared Responsibility**: Distributive Leadership recognizes that leadership is not confined to a single individual but is a collective responsibility shared among multiple members of a team or organization. This principle emphasizes that leadership can emerge from anyone, regardless of their formal position or title within the organization. Shared responsibility encourages a sense of ownership and accountability among

team members, as they understand that they all play a role in driving the success of the organization.

2. **Collaborative Decision-Making**: At the heart of Distributive Leadership is the belief in collaborative decision-making. Leaders across different levels and functions collaborate to exchange ideas, perspectives, and expertise when making decisions. This collaborative approach ensures that diverse viewpoints are considered, leading to more informed and effective decisions. By involving stakeholders in the decision-making process, Distributive Leadership promotes buy-in and commitment to the chosen course of action.

3. **Empowerment and Trust**: Distributive Leadership empowers individuals to take initiative and make decisions within their areas of expertise. Leaders trust their team members to act autonomously and responsibly, creating a culture of empowerment and accountability. This trust is essential for fostering innovation, creativity, and a sense of ownership among team members. Empowered employees are more engaged, motivated, and committed to achieving organizational goals.

4. **Adaptability and Flexibility**: In today's rapidly changing business environment, Distributive Leadership enables organizations to be adaptable and flexible in responding to challenges and opportunities. By decentralizing decision-making authority, organizations can quickly adapt to changing circumstances and seize new opportunities as they arise. Distributive Leadership encourages leaders and teams to be agile and responsive, enabling them to navigate uncertainty and complexity effectively.

5. **Continuous Learning and Development**: Distributive Leadership promotes a culture of continuous learning and development. Leaders are committed to supporting the growth and development of their team members through mentorship, coaching, and providing opportunities for skill-building and professional growth. This focus on development not only enhances individual capabilities but also strengthens the overall leadership capacity of the organization. Continuous learning ensures that leaders and teams stay ahead of the curve in a rapidly evolving business landscape.

6. **Inclusive and Diverse Perspectives**: Distributive Leadership leverages the diverse perspectives and experiences of team members to drive innovation and problem-solving. By involving leaders from various backgrounds, cultures, and disciplines, organizations can tap into a wealth of ideas and insights. This inclusivity fosters a culture of respect, collaboration, and appreciation for diversity within the organization, leading to better decision-making and outcomes. Inclusive and diverse perspectives ensure that the organization remains relevant and responsive to the needs of its stakeholders.

In summary, the six fundamental principles of Distributive Leadership framework emphasize the importance of shared responsibility, collaborative decision-making, empowerment, adaptability, continuous learning, and inclusive perspectives in driving organizational success. By embracing these principles, organizations can foster a culture of leadership excellence, where every member feels valued, engaged, and empowered to contribute to the collective goals of the organization.

What motivates individuals to adopt a Distributive approach to leadership

Several factors can motivate individuals to adopt a Distributive approach to leadership:

1. **Desire for Inclusivity**: Distributive Leadership recognizes the value of diversity and inclusivity in driving organizational success. Leaders who prioritize inclusivity understand that diverse teams are more creative, innovative, and effective in problem-solving. By adopting a Distributive approach, leaders signal their commitment to creating an inclusive culture where every team member's voice is heard and valued. This fosters a sense of belonging and psychological safety, encouraging team members to contribute their unique perspectives and talents without fear of judgment or exclusion.

2. **Recognition of Collective Wisdom**: One of the key principles of Distributive Leadership is the belief in the collective wisdom of the team. Leaders who embrace this approach understand that no single individual possesses all the knowledge or expertise needed to address complex challenges effectively. Instead, they value the diverse experiences, skills, and insights of their team members. By distributing leadership responsibilities, leaders tap into the collective intelligence of the group, leading to better decision-making and more innovative solutions. This fosters a culture of collaboration and mutual respect, where team members feel empowered to share their ideas and collaborate towards shared goals.

3. **Promotion of Empowerment**: Empowerment is a central tenet of Distributive Leadership. Leaders who adopt this approach prioritize giving their team members autonomy

and decision-making authority within their areas of expertise. By empowering team members to take ownership of their work, leaders foster a sense of accountability and ownership, motivating individuals to go above and beyond in their roles. This empowerment also builds trust between leaders and team members, creating a positive work environment where individuals feel valued, respected, and motivated to contribute their best efforts.

4. **Adaptability to Change**: In today's rapidly changing business landscape, adaptability is essential for organizational success. Leaders who embrace Distributive Leadership understand that centralized decision-making can hinder agility and responsiveness to change. By distributing leadership responsibilities, leaders empower teams to make decisions quickly and adapt to changing circumstances. This flexibility allows organizations to seize new opportunities and navigate challenges more effectively, ensuring their long-term viability and competitiveness in the marketplace.

5. **Commitment to Continuous Learning**: Distributive Leadership promotes a culture of continuous learning and development. Leaders who prioritize learning understand that knowledge and skills are essential for individual and organizational growth. By embracing a Distributive approach, leaders create opportunities for team members to learn from one another, share best practices, and develop new skills. This commitment to learning fosters a culture of innovation and improvement, where individuals are encouraged to seek out new challenges and stretch their capabilities to achieve their full potential.

6. **Desire for Innovation**: Innovation thrives in environments where diverse perspectives are encouraged and valued. Leaders who adopt Distributive Leadership recognize that innovation is essential for organizational success and growth. By distributing leadership responsibilities and empowering team members to contribute their ideas and insights, leaders create fertile ground for innovation to flourish. This fosters a culture of experimentation, creativity, and risk-taking, where individuals feel empowered to explore new ideas and challenge the status quo. As a result, organizations can stay ahead of the curve and drive sustainable growth in an increasingly competitive marketplace.

In summary, the motivations for adopting a Distributive approach to leadership are rooted in the desire to create inclusive, empowering, adaptable, and innovative organizations that can thrive in today's complex and dynamic business environment. By embracing Distributive Leadership, leaders can unleash the full potential of their teams, foster a culture of collaboration and continuous learning, and drive long-term success and sustainability for their organizations.

Manifestation of Distributive Leadership framework in Day-to-Day Leadership Practices

The manifestation of Distributive Leadership framework in day-to-day leadership practices can be observed through various actions and behaviors that reflect the principles and values inherent in this approach. Here are some examples of how Distributive Leadership manifests in everyday leadership practices:

1. **Delegating Authority**: Distributive leaders delegate authority and decision-making responsibilities to team members based on their expertise and capabilities. Instead of micromanaging

every aspect of a project, they empower team members to take ownership of their tasks and make decisions autonomously. This delegation of authority not only frees up the leader's time but also fosters a sense of accountability and ownership among team members.

2. **Encouraging Collaboration**: Distributive leaders promote collaboration and teamwork by creating opportunities for team members to work together towards common goals. They encourage open communication, idea sharing, and knowledge exchange among team members, fostering a culture of collaboration and mutual support. By valuing and leveraging the diverse perspectives and talents of their team, distributive leaders enhance creativity, innovation, and problem-solving capabilities within the organization.

3. **Providing Support and Resources**: Distributive leaders support their team members by providing them with the resources, tools, and support they need to succeed. Whether it's providing access to training and development opportunities, offering mentorship and coaching, or removing obstacles and barriers to success, distributive leaders prioritize the well-being and growth of their team members. This support creates a positive work environment where individuals feel valued, motivated, and empowered to achieve their goals.

4. **Promoting Inclusivity and Diversity**: Distributive leaders promote inclusivity and diversity within their teams and organizations by valuing and respecting the unique perspectives, backgrounds, and experiences of their team members. They actively seek out diverse viewpoints and encourage participation from all members of the team, regardless of their position or background. By fostering an

inclusive and diverse work environment, distributive leaders create opportunities for innovation, creativity, and growth within the organization.

5. **Facilitating Continuous Learning and Development**: Distributive leaders prioritize continuous learning and development by creating opportunities for skill-building, knowledge sharing, and professional growth within their teams. They encourage team members to pursue learning opportunities, attend training sessions, and seek out new challenges that stretch their capabilities. By investing in the development of their team members, distributive leaders ensure that their organization remains agile, adaptable, and competitive in a rapidly changing business environment.

6. **Celebrating Successes and Acknowledging Contributions**: Distributive leaders celebrate successes and acknowledge the contributions of their team members. They recognize and reward individuals for their hard work, creativity, and achievements, fostering a culture of appreciation and recognition within the organization. By publicly acknowledging and celebrating successes, distributive leaders inspire motivation, loyalty, and commitment among team members, driving continued excellence and performance within the organization.

In summary, Distributive Leadership manifests in day-to-day leadership practices through actions and behaviors that prioritize empowerment, collaboration, inclusivity, continuous learning, and recognition of contributions. By embracing the principles of Distributive Leadership, leaders can create high-performing teams and organizations that are agile, adaptable, and poised for long-term success in today's complex and dynamic business environment.

Real Life Examples Illustrating Leaders who Exemplify Distributive Leadership Framework

Real-life examples provide tangible illustrations of how Distributive Leadership principles can be applied in various contexts. Here are few examples showcasing practical applications of the Distributive Leadership framework:

1. **Google:**

   - ***Example***: Google's approach to distributive leadership is ingrained in its organizational culture, which emphasizes collaboration, innovation, and employee empowerment. The company's founders, Larry Page and Sergey Brin, envisioned Google as a place where employees could pursue ambitious projects and contribute ideas regardless of their position within the company.

   - ***Application***: At Google, distributive leadership manifests in several ways. For instance, the company's open-office layout and informal communication channels facilitate collaboration among teams. Google also encourages employees to participate in decision-making through forums like "TGIF" meetings, where anyone can ask questions or share ideas with senior leadership. Additionally, initiatives like the "20% time" policy allow employees to allocate a portion of their workweek to pursue passion projects, fostering a culture of autonomy and innovation.

   - ***Impact***: Google's distributive leadership approach has been instrumental in driving innovation and maintaining a competitive edge in the technology industry. By empowering employees to take ownership of projects and pursue their interests, Google has fostered a culture of creativity and experimentation that has led to the development of groundbreaking products and services, such as Gmail, Google Maps, and Android.

2. **Nordstrom**:

- ***Example***: Nordstrom's distributive leadership model is rooted in its commitment to delivering exceptional customer service and fostering a culture of empowerment among its employees. The company's decentralized approach to leadership allows frontline staff to make decisions autonomously and tailor their service approach to meet customer needs effectively.

- ***Application***: In Nordstrom's retail stores, distributive leadership is evident in various aspects of operations. For example, sales associates are empowered to make decisions regarding customer interactions, such as handling returns, resolving complaints, and personalizing recommendations. Store managers also have the autonomy to implement strategies that align with their store's unique characteristics and customer base. Additionally, Nordstrom's "no-hierarchy" culture encourages open communication and collaboration among employees at all levels.

- ***Impact***: Nordstrom's distributive leadership philosophy has contributed to its reputation for providing exceptional customer service and building strong customer loyalty. By empowering frontline staff to take ownership of customer interactions and make decisions independently, Nordstrom has created a customer-centric culture that prioritizes responsiveness, personalization, and satisfaction. This approach has been instrumental in differentiating Nordstrom from competitors and driving customer retention and loyalty over the years.

3. **Semco Partners:**

- **Example:** Semco Partners, a Brazilian conglomerate, is renowned for its innovative approach to organizational structure and leadership under the guidance of Ricardo Semler. Semler transformed Semco from a traditional hierarchical organization into a decentralized, democratic workplace where employees have a significant say in decision-making.

- **Application:** At Semco, distributive leadership is embedded in the company's DNA. Employees have the freedom to choose their leaders, set their own schedules, and participate in decision-making processes through democratic forums. Semler introduced radical practices such as open-book management, where financial information is shared transparently with employees, and participatory budgeting, where teams have autonomy over budget allocation.

- **Impact:** The distributive leadership model at Semco has led to remarkable outcomes. Employee engagement and job satisfaction are high, leading to lower turnover rates and increased productivity. The company's revenue and profitability have also flourished, showcasing how a decentralized leadership approach can foster innovation, agility, and resilience in the face of change.

4. **W.L. Gore & Associates:**

- *Example:* W.L. Gore & Associates, a global materials science company, operates on a lattice organizational structure that epitomizes distributive leadership principles. Founded by Bill Gore, the company values employee autonomy, collaboration, and innovation.

- ***Application***: Distributive leadership is deeply ingrained in Gore's culture. The company operates without traditional hierarchies or formal titles, and decisions are made collaboratively by small, self-managed teams. Employees have the freedom to pursue projects they are passionate about, and leadership emerges organically based on expertise and contribution.

- ***Impact***: Gore's distributive leadership model has yielded remarkable results. The company has a track record of innovation, with products ranging from GORE-TEX fabric to medical devices. Employee satisfaction and engagement are high, leading to long tenures and a strong sense of commitment to the company's mission. By decentralizing leadership and empowering employees, Gore has built a resilient and adaptive organization capable of thriving in dynamic market conditions.

Strategies for cultivating Distributive Leadership framework approach in leadership

Cultivating a Distributive Leadership framework approach involves intentional efforts to develop and reinforce key behaviors and principles that align with this leadership style. Here are strategies for cultivating Distributive Leadership within an organization:

1. **Leadership Development Programs**: Leadership development programs should be comprehensive and tailored to the organization's needs. They can include workshops, seminars, coaching sessions, and mentorship programs focused on Distributive Leadership principles. These

programs should educate leaders about shared responsibility, collaborative decision-making, empowerment, and fostering inclusivity.

2. **Modeling Distributive Leadership Behaviors**: Leaders must lead by example and demonstrate Distributive Leadership behaviors in their interactions with team members. This involves being open to diverse perspectives, sharing power and decision-making authority, and promoting collaboration and inclusivity. Leaders should actively seek input from team members, listen attentively, and incorporate their ideas into decision-making processes.

3. **Encouraging Autonomy and Accountability**: Empowering team members involves giving them autonomy to make decisions within their areas of expertise. Leaders should provide clear expectations and guidelines while allowing individuals the freedom to execute tasks in their own way. Alongside autonomy, fostering a culture of accountability ensures that team members take ownership of their work and actions, leading to higher performance and engagement.

4. **Creating Opportunities for Collaboration**: Collaboration should be actively encouraged and facilitated within the organization. Leaders can organize cross-functional projects, brainstorming sessions, and team-building activities to promote collaboration among team members. Providing platforms for knowledge sharing and communication, such as team meetings, collaboration tools, and networking events, also fosters a collaborative work environment.

5. **Providing Feedback and Recognition**: Regular feedback and recognition are essential for cultivating a Distributive

Leadership culture. Leaders should provide constructive feedback to help individuals learn and grow, while also recognizing and celebrating their achievements. This fosters a positive work environment where team members feel valued and motivated to contribute their best efforts.

6. **Promoting Inclusivity and Diversity**: Inclusivity and diversity should be embraced and promoted at all levels of the organization. Leaders can create diverse teams, encourage diverse perspectives, and ensure equal opportunities for all team members. Establishing inclusive policies and practices, such as flexible work arrangements and diversity training programs, also helps create a more inclusive workplace culture.

7. **Supporting Continuous Learning and Development**: Investing in the continuous learning and development of team members is crucial for their growth and success. Leaders should provide access to training programs, workshops, and resources that enhance individuals' skills and knowledge. Encouraging a growth mindset and providing opportunities for stretch assignments and career advancement also fosters continuous learning and development.

8. **Establishing Clear Expectations and Goals**: Clear communication of organizational goals and expectations is essential for alignment and accountability. Leaders should ensure that team members understand their roles, responsibilities, and performance expectations. By setting clear goals and objectives that support the organization's vision, leaders empower individuals to contribute meaningfully to the achievement of shared goals.

9. **Creating a Feedback-Rich Culture**: A feedback-rich culture promotes open communication and continuous

improvement. Leaders should encourage regular feedback exchanges between team members and provide opportunities for constructive feedback and dialogue. Creating a safe and supportive environment where feedback is valued and acted upon fosters trust and collaboration among team members.

10. **Leading by Example**: Ultimately, leaders must lead by example and embody the principles of Distributive Leadership in their own actions and behaviors. This involves being transparent, collaborative, and inclusive in decision-making processes. By demonstrating a commitment to empowerment, collaboration, and continuous learning, leaders inspire trust and confidence in their teams and set the tone for a positive and productive work culture.

By implementing these strategies, organizations can cultivate a culture of Distributive Leadership that empowers and engages team members, fosters collaboration and innovation, and drives organizational success and resilience.

Distributive Leadership – My Observation and Experience

In the bustling corridors of a multinational corporation, I once had the privilege of witnessing firsthand the transformative power of Distributive Leadership in action. The story I'm about to share unfolded during a critical period of change within the organization, when a new project was launched to revamp the company's outdated customer service processes.

At the helm of this ambitious project was Sarah, the newly appointed project manager. With her natural charisma and collaborative approach, Sarah embodied the principles of Distributive Leadership, setting the stage for a remarkable journey ahead.

As the project kicked off, Sarah wasted no time in assembling a diverse team comprising individuals from different departments and levels of seniority. She believed that harnessing the collective expertise and perspectives of the team members would be crucial for the project's success.

Instead of dictating the project roadmap herself, Sarah adopted a participative approach, encouraging team members to contribute their ideas and insights during brainstorming sessions and strategy meetings. She recognized that each team member brought valuable expertise to the table and empowered them to take ownership of various aspects of the project.

One of the key decisions Sarah made early on was to delegate specific responsibilities to different team members based on their strengths and areas of expertise. She believed in the power of autonomy and accountability, trusting her team members to execute their tasks effectively while providing support and guidance whenever needed.

Throughout the project, Sarah fostered a culture of open communication and collaboration, creating opportunities for team members to share their progress, raise concerns, and brainstorm solutions collectively. She encouraged healthy debates and welcomed diverse viewpoints, believing that constructive conflict could lead to better outcomes.

As the project progressed, Sarah ensured that team members received regular feedback and recognition for their contributions. She celebrated small wins along the way and provided constructive feedback to help team members learn and grow. By acknowledging their efforts and achievements, Sarah motivated her team to stay committed and focused on the shared goal.

Despite facing inevitable challenges and setbacks along the way, Sarah remained resilient and optimistic, inspiring her team to persevere through adversity. She remained transparent and honest in her communication, addressing any concerns or obstacles promptly and proactively.

In the end, Sarah's Distributive Leadership approach paid off handsomely as the project culminated in a successful rollout of the new customer service processes. The project team not only achieved their objectives but also emerged stronger and more cohesive than ever before.

Reflecting on Sarah's leadership journey, I couldn't help but marvel at the profound impact of Distributive Leadership in driving positive change and fostering collaboration within the organization. Sarah's ability to empower her team, promote inclusivity, and facilitate open communication exemplified the core principles of Distributive Leadership, leaving a lasting impression on all who had the privilege of working alongside her.

As I witnessed this remarkable transformation unfold, it reinforced my belief in the power of Distributive Leadership to inspire greatness and drive organizational success in today's complex and dynamic business environment.

Conclusion

In the captivating journey through the Distributive Leadership framework, we've explored the profound impact of empowering leadership, collaboration, and inclusivity within organizations. Through the lens of real-world experiences and insights, we've witnessed how Distributive Leadership can inspire teams to achieve remarkable results and foster a culture of shared ownership and accountability.

As we conclude this chapter, it's evident that Distributive Leadership isn't just a leadership style; it's a philosophy that champions the belief in the collective wisdom and potential of every team member. By embracing Distributive Leadership principles, organizations can unlock new levels of innovation, resilience, and engagement, driving sustainable success in today's rapidly evolving business landscape.

In the story we've shared, we saw how Sarah's Distributive Leadership approach transformed a challenging project into a triumph of collaboration and collective achievement. Her ability to empower her team, promote inclusivity, and foster open communication set a shining example of Distributive Leadership in action.

In embracing Distributive Leadership, we not only unlock the full potential of our teams but also cultivate a culture of trust, innovation, and resilience that propels organizations towards enduring success. Together, let us embark on this journey of leadership transformation, guided by the timeless principles of Distributive Leadership.

Practical Exercises and Reflection Questions

These exercises and reflection questions are designed to encourage readers to actively apply and critically reflect on the concepts discussed in this chapter. They aim to bridge the gap between theory and practical application, fostering a deeper understanding of how leadership frameworks can be valuable tools in real-world leadership scenarios.

Practical Exercises:

1. **Team Collaboration Simulation**: Divide the participants into small groups and present them with a hypothetical project scenario. Encourage them to apply Distributive Leadership principles to plan, execute, and evaluate the project collaboratively within their groups.

2. **Leadership Role-Play**: Organize a role-playing activity where participants take on different leadership roles within a team setting. Encourage them to demonstrate Distributive Leadership behaviors such as empowerment, inclusivity, and collaborative decision-making.

3. **Case Study Analysis**: Provide participants with case studies of real-world organizations that have successfully implemented Distributive Leadership practices. Ask them to analyze the key strategies employed by these organizations and identify lessons that can be applied to their own leadership contexts.

4. **Team Building Exercise**: Facilitate a team-building exercise where participants participate in collaborative activities such as problem-solving challenges, group discussions, or team-building games. Encourage them to reflect on how Distributive Leadership principles can enhance teamwork and foster a positive team dynamic.

Reflection Questions:

1. **Personal Leadership Style**: Reflect on your own leadership style and approach. How do you currently empower and engage your team members? In what ways can you incorporate Distributive Leadership principles to enhance your leadership effectiveness?

2. **Team Dynamics**: Consider the dynamics within your team or organization. How do team members collaborate and communicate with each other? Are there opportunities to promote inclusivity, diversity, and shared decision-making within your team?

3. **Challenges and Opportunities**: Identify any challenges or barriers that may hinder the implementation of Distributive Leadership practices within your organization. How can you overcome these challenges and leverage opportunities to foster a culture of Distributive Leadership?

4. **Impact on Organizational Culture**: Reflect on the potential impact of adopting Distributive Leadership principles on your organization's culture and performance. How can Distributive Leadership contribute to creating a more innovative, resilient, and engaged workforce?

5. **Continuous Improvement**: Consider ways to continuously improve your leadership effectiveness and promote Distributive Leadership within your team or organization. What steps can you take to cultivate a culture of empowerment, collaboration, and inclusivity in your leadership practices?

Chapter 14

Building your Unique Leadership Perspective

In this final chapter, we culminate our journey of leadership exploration by reflecting on the profound insights gained from traversing the diverse landscape of leadership frameworks. As we stand at the culmination of our odyssey, it is essential to acknowledge the transformative nature of our collective experience and the invaluable lessons learned along the way. Throughout our exploration, we have delved deep into the intricacies of various leadership frameworks, from the traditional to the contemporary, uncovering the underlying principles, practical applications, and real-world examples that define each framework. Now, armed with a comprehensive understanding of the multifaceted nature of leadership, we turn our gaze inward, focusing on the synthesis of our learnings and the cultivation of our unique leadership perspective.

As we wrap up our exploration, let's reflect on the key practical takeaways from each leadership framework discussed and consider how we can build our unique leadership perspective.

1. **Great Man Theory:**

    - Recognize the impact of individual leaders in shaping history and organizational outcomes.
    - Embrace the potential within yourself to make a difference, regardless of your background or circumstances.

2. **Trait Theory:**

    - Identify and develop key leadership traits and attributes within yourself and your team.
    - Foster a growth mindset and invest in continuous self-improvement to enhance your leadership capabilities.

3. **Behavioral Theories:**

    - Focus on observable behaviors and actions to drive effective leadership practices.
    - Lead by example, demonstrating the behaviors and values you wish to see in your team and organization.

4. **Contingency Theories:**

    - Adapt your leadership approach to fit the unique demands of each situation and context.
    - Remain flexible and open-minded, willing to adjust your strategies based on changing circumstances and needs.

5. **Transformational Leadership:**

    - Inspire and empower others to reach their full potential, fostering a culture of growth and innovation.
    - Lead with authenticity, passion, and vision to drive meaningful change and organizational success.

6. **Transactional Leadership:**

    - Establish clear expectations, provide rewards and incentives for performance, and maintain accountability.
    - Balance transactional practices with a focus on building trust, relationships, and shared goals with your team.

7. **Servant Leadership:**

   - Prioritize the needs of others, foster collaboration, and empower individuals to achieve their goals.
   - Lead with humility, empathy, and compassion, creating a supportive environment where everyone can thrive.

8. **Authentic Leadership:**

   - Lead with integrity, transparency, and self-awareness, staying true to your values and principles.
   - Build trust and credibility through genuine connections and honest communication with your team.

9. **Situational Leadership:**

   - Adapt your leadership style to the readiness and development level of your team members.
   - Provide tailored support, guidance, and direction based on individual needs and circumstances.

10. **Charismatic Leadership:**

    - Inspire and motivate others through your compelling vision, enthusiasm, and personal charisma.
    - Cultivate your communication and storytelling skills to effectively convey your message and rally others around your cause.

11. **Leader-Member Exchange (LMX) Theory:**

    - Foster high-quality relationships with all team members, promoting trust, respect, and mutual support.
    - Invest time and effort in building rapport and understanding individual needs and aspirations.

12. **Distributed Leadership**:

- Encourage shared leadership and collaboration across all levels of the organization.
- Empower individuals to take ownership of their roles and contribute to collective goals and outcomes.

In our leadership journey, it's crucial to recognize that while understanding various frameworks is essential, effective leadership goes beyond simply adhering to a set of principles or models. It's about embracing adaptability, creativity, and empathy to navigate the complexities of the modern world. As a leader, we must continuously evolve and refine our approach, drawing from the wisdom of various frameworks while remaining agile and responsive to the unique needs and challenges of our team and organization.

The dynamic and ever-changing nature of the world demands leaders who can not only understand and apply different leadership theories but also innovate and adapt in the face of uncertainty. Embracing diversity of thought, fostering a culture of inclusion, and encouraging creativity and experimentation are essential aspects of modern leadership. By embracing a growth mindset and a commitment to lifelong learning, we can stay ahead of the curve and lead with confidence and resilience.

Moreover, effective leadership is not just about achieving individual success but also about empowering others to reach their full potential. As we cultivate our unique leadership perspective, remember the importance of building strong relationships, fostering trust, and empowering those around us. By investing in the growth and development of our team members, we can create a positive and inclusive work environment where everyone feels valued, supported, and inspired to excel.

Furthermore, leadership is not a solo journey but a collaborative effort that requires the collective contributions of a diverse team. By embracing distributed leadership principles and encouraging shared decision-making and accountability, we can harness the collective intelligence and creativity of our team members to drive innovation and achieve shared goals. By leveraging the strengths and expertise of each individual, we can create a high-performing team that is greater than the sum of its parts.

In closing, I encourage the reader to embrace your role as a leader with humility, integrity, and a deep sense of purpose. Your journey as a leader will be characterized by challenges, triumphs, and moments of profound growth. Approach each experience with an open mind and a willingness to learn, recognizing that true leadership greatness is not measured by the title you hold, but by the positive impact you have on the lives of those around you. Let us continue to embark on this journey of leadership excellence together, striving to make a meaningful difference in the world, one step at a time.